Roger G. Sweeney

Macaws

Everything about Purchase, Management, Housing,
Feeding, Health Care, and Breeding

With a Special Chapter on Understanding Macaws and
Profiles of the Species

35 Drawings by Michele Earle-Bridges
and 20 Color Photographs

© Copyright 1992 by Barron's Educational Series, Inc.

All inquiries should be addressed to:
Barron's Educational Series, Inc.
250 Wireless Boulevard
Hauppauge, New York 11788

International Standard Book No. 0-8120-4768-0

Library of Congress Catalog Card No. 91-40719

Library of Congress Cataloging-in-Publication Data

Sweeney, Roger G.
   Macaws / Roger G. Sweeney ; drawings by Michele Earle-Bridges.
      p. cm.
   Includes index.
   ISBN 0-8120-4768-0
   1. Macaws.   I. Title
SF473.M33S94   1992
636.6'865—dc20   91-40719
                            CIP

PRINTED IN HONG KONG

6 7 8 9 0   4900   12 11 10 9 8 7

About the author:

Roger G. Sweeney is Livestock Manager of Birdworld Bird Park, the largest public bird gardens in the United Kingdom. During the past five years he has worked with and bred most of the commonly seen *Ara* species, as well as the rarer species such as the hyacinthine macaw. A member of several avicultural societies, he lectures on psittacine management and has written books and magazine articles on the subject.

Photos on the covers:

Front cover: Blue and gold macaw *(Ara ararauna)*.
Inside front cover: Yellow-collared macaw *(Ara auricollis)*.
Inside back cover: Green winged macaw *(Ara chloroptera)*.
Back cover: Top left: Blue and Gold macaw *(Ara ararauna)*; top right: Scarlet macaws *(Ara macao)*; bottom left: Hyacinthine macaw *(Anodorhynchus hyacinthinus)*; bottom right: Severe macaw *(Ara severa)*.

Photo credits:

Gary W. Ellis: civ, top left. Roger G. Sweeney: pages 10; 63, bottom; civ, top right and bottom left. Matthew M. Vriends: front cover; pages 9, top left; 64; ciii. B. Everett Webb: cii; pages 9, top right, bottom; 27; 28; 45; 46; 63, top; civ, bottom right .

Note and Warning:

People who suffer from allergies to feathers or any kind of feather dust should not keep macaws. In case of doubt, check with the doctor before you acquire one.

In dealing with macaws, one may receive injuries from bites or scratches. Have such wounds attended to by a doctor. Although psittacosis (parrot fever) is not among the commonly seen illnesses of macaws (see page 39), it can produce symptoms in both humans and parrots that may be life-threatening. At any sign of a cold or flu, see a doctor immediately.

Contents

Preface

Macaws have been kept in captivity for many decades. Their beauty and charisma is outstanding, and anyone working with psittacines must surely hold a special place in their hearts for these, the largest of living parrots.

Today, with increasing pressures on the wild populations of a majority of macaw species, the need for captive breeding and better management of all birds held in captivity is of prime importance. Only the dedication of aviculturists can maintain a strong, self-sustaining population of these beautiful birds in captivity without the need to take more birds from the wild.

Most of my time as Livestock Manager at Birdworld Bird Park, Farnham, England, is spent on the management of bird breeding programs, breeding loans, exchanges, and stud books. However, Birdworld has long recognized the importance of private aviculture and has for many years held an annual avicultural day. A full schedule of events includes displays and talks dedicated to improving the care and breeding of the many birds held by private collectors. Today, improving the understanding of the many people who visit the collection each year has become an ongoing service at Birdworld.

All parrots, particularly the larger macaws, are among the most demanding birds that can be kept as pets. Naturally, the needs of these birds should not be overlooked while concentrating on their breeding programs. Many thousands of parrots are kept as pets in the United Kingdom. In America, this figure probably reaches into the millions. The chance to improve the care of these birds in captivity should not be lost by professionals as they concentrate purely on breeding. I hope that the information in this book will prove of use to anyone who has a pet macaw. If the care of any captive macaws improves because of this book, then it will have been well worthwhile.

If any questions arise from the reading of this book, or if there are points that are not covered, I would be glad to try to provide answers. Please write to me in care of the publisher and I will respond individually.

Roger G. Sweeney
Birdworld Bird Park
Farnham, England

Understanding Macaws

What Is a Macaw?

Macaws are among the most striking members of the parrot family (Psittacidae). They come from Central and South America and have been widely kept as pets since the beginning of the century. Some records suggest that green-winged macaws were being kept as long ago as the turn of the seventeenth century.

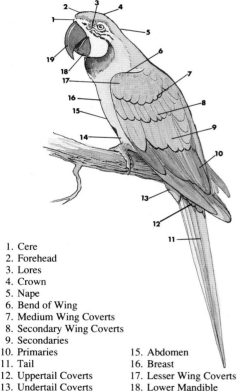

1. Cere
2. Forehead
3. Lores
4. Crown
5. Nape
6. Bend of Wing
7. Medium Wing Coverts
8. Secondary Wing Coverts
9. Secondaries

10. Primaries	15. Abdomen
11. Tail	16. Breast
12. Uppertail Coverts	17. Lesser Wing Coverts
13. Undertail Coverts	18. Lower Mandible
14. Thigh	19. Upper Mandible

Topography of the macaw showing the names of various parts of the body. Knowing the correct term to describe a feature can be of great benefit when seeking advice from a veterinarian.

The early years of the twentieth century saw several macaw species become widely available and many first recorded breedings stem from this time. However, because of problems in accurately sexing these birds (all macaws are sexually monomorphic) and because until fairly recently the majority of macaws entering the country were being sold individually and kept alone as pets, few attempts were made to breed them.

The macaw group today consists of 17 living species, which are divided into three genera. Although the various species vary greatly in size and coloration, all share the same basic physical characteristics. All are known for their long tails, slim bodies, and broad heads, but it is the large macaws such as the scarlet and the blue and gold that are instantly recognizable to most people because of their imposing size and vivid coloration. The

The main flight feathers are divided into the ten outer feathers called primaries, and the ten inner feathers called secondaries.

1. Primaries	5. Primaries
2. Spurious Wing	6. Secondaries
3. Middle or Lesser Coverts	7. Tertiaries
4. Scapulars	

Understanding Macaws

The skeleton of a macaw.

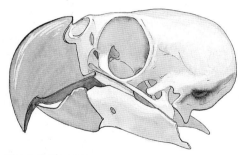

The skull of a macaw.

smaller species, although physically similar, are fairly dull by comparison and are less likely to be recognized at first sight.

Of the three genera of macaws, the genus *Ara* contains 13 of the 17 known living species and these 13 include most of the species that are likely to be seen in captivity. Only *Ara* species should be considered as pets. The four remaining species, three of them from the genus *Anodorhynchus* (the hyacinthine, glaucous, and Lear's macaws—the latter is sometimes commonly known as the blue macaw), and the exceptionally rare Spix's macaw

of the monotypic genus *Cyanopsitta* are all so rare that every bird in captivity will be needed for breeding stock if these birds are to survive for future generations to see and appreciate them. (Note: Some authorities place Hahn's and the noble macaw in the genus *Diopsittaca*.)

Voice and Mimicry

Unlike the Amazon parrots, with whom they often share their range, macaws in their wild state are not great mimics. Vocal expression is mainly used in group situations with birds of their own or similar species. Also unlike Amazons, macaws only use their natural voice, which does not vary greatly in its sound and pitch.

Vocal expression within a group of macaws is not complex. The distinctive cry of the adult macaw, which is instantly recognizable to those birds nearby, is used for calling and for recognition. Variations in volume, harshness, and in the call itself, are used by macaws to convey several separate recognizable signals, including danger, distress, food, aggression, courtship, recognition of another bird, and affection.

In captivity, however, both wild-caught and captive-bred birds will seek to interact with their owners once a relationship of trust has been established. In addition to seeking physical contact, most birds will try to imitate the sounds and movements of their owners. With patience, these early attempts at mimicry can be developed until certain words are imitated almost perfectly. Once begun, mimicry will without doubt be continued as this will prove an excellent way for the bird to attract attention. Mimicry can also help keep a macaw interested when there is nothing else for it to do. A tape player or even a radio can keep a bird entertained for hours. Macaws already used to mimicking find this quite stimulating. They may even pick up new words from such listening sessions, though most of the radio dialogue is probably spoken too quickly for the bird to absorb it.

Understanding Macaws

Macaws vocalize to call each other—or their owner.

Handling and Temperament

As strongly suggested throughout this book, only hand-reared macaws should be considered as prospective pet birds. Wild-caught birds never completely adapt to a household environment and frequently engage in screaming bouts that are certain to test the patience of even the most devoted of owners. Moreover, wild-caught birds can never be as tame or confiding as hand-reared birds, which come in contact with humans from the very start of their lives.

When reared artificially, young macaws are generally unafraid of human contact. Nevertheless, a macaw that is within its first year of life when it is received from the breeder will need some time to accept its new owner. Often these birds are strongly attached to the person who has reared them and have had little or no contact with other people. For the young bird, a change in owner usually means a simultaneous move to a new and unfamiliar home. It is not surprising, then, that young macaws when first arriving in their new environment seem totally disoriented and often become extremely shy and nervous. They will need reassurance and patient handling during the first few weeks, but once the birds become confident of their new owner and surroundings they should soon lose all nervousness and regain all their tameness and inquisitiveness.

Once a trusting relationship has been established with the macaw, as much time as possible should be spent playing with it. In the wild, macaws are quite affectionate and use much of their resting time to socialize by preening one another. In captivity, the owner is the bird's only source of affection; therefore, it will need as much attention as the owner can give.

Always handle macaws with confidence. It should be remembered that hand-reared macaws never develop a "natural" fear of people. As it grows into adolescence, such a macaw can become boisterous, mischievous, and difficult to handle. In this event, the owner should react with confidence at all times to keep the bird's respect. Any signs of weakness will be tested in full. If not kept in line, such a bird can go on to become totally untrustworthy as a pet and may need to be confined to its cage. Never allow bad behavior to develop, but if it does, then reserve this macaw only for breeding and try again with another young bird.

Macaws in Nature

In nature, macaws live and behave differently than they do in captivity. This is not really surprising as no captive enclosure could ever come close to recreating their natural surroundings. Although a wild macaw's home range can cover an extremely large area, macaws are adaptable: In captivity, they readily accept the facilities and life-style that are available to them. Captive life is neither better nor worse than the life macaws would have in their wild state, but it is certainly not the same. Some aspects of their natural history are described below; but to completely understand macaws, they must be observed first-hand in their natural setting.

Movement

In captivity macaws are great climbers. They often clamber upside down across the roof of their

Understanding Macaws

A group of macaws in the wild socializing and preening each other.

enclosure and perform great acrobatics, such as hanging by one toe while spinning around to look at something. In aviaries nearly all the bird's movements involve climbing, especially in a well-perched aviary where the macaw is able to reach every important area of its enclosure from a nearby perch. Hence, a bird keeper who has never enjoyed the opportunity to observe macaws in nature is likely to assume that much of their movement in the wild is undertaken in the same way. Certainly, a macaw seen awkwardly walking along the floor, all feet and bill, will also lead the observer to conclude that they are predominantly a climbing bird, and perhaps even to believe them capable only of restricted flight. Of course, nothing could be further from the truth.

Macaws in their wild state are great flying birds. Once a macaw has taken to the air, with legs neatly folded back, head held out straight, and long wings extended, it reveals itself as a powerful and elegant flying bird. Macaws can easily cover many miles while in flight with seemingly little effort or strain; they do, of course, still climb once they have landed

in the top of a tree to get to the particular area of the tree they want to reach. In contrast to captive birds that walk the short distances between two adjoining branches, wild macaws nearly always resort to flying.

Habitat and Range

Preferred habitats vary among the seventeen different species of macaws, as do distributions and altitudes at which they can be encountered. To generalize, macaws favor undisturbed, lowland, humid forests, such as those that covered much of South America but that in recent times have been dramatically reduced. Some species can be found at higher altitudes, however, and others in more open woodlands and forest edges. The military macaw lives in quite arid regions across much of its range. Undisturbed forests however are essential to the lives of wild macaws. As already mentioned, the natural range for a wild macaw is quite extensive because macaws are strong flyers that will travel widely to find the best food supplies or nest sites. In some species there is clear evidence of seasonal migration across some parts of their range. Thus, it is clear that in the long term, populations of macaws cannot survive in isolated parks or regions of forests. They will require large undisturbed areas of primary forest to thrive.

Food

The foods eaten by the different species of macaws vary greatly according to the particular species, the region each inhabits, and the foods that are available throughout the year. Some points, however, are clear. First, in the wild birds need to

Top left and right: Green-winged macaws *(Ara chloroptera)* like all macaws are natural climbers. If kept in an outdoor aviary, they will take full advantage of whatever trees and branches are provided for them. ▶
Bottom: A pair of green-winged macaws.

eat more food daily than captive macaws because the former spend greater amounts of energy throughout the course of the day in flying about in search of food. Second, most wild foods macaws eat are low in nutritional value—though opportunist food supplies, such as carrion, will be readily eaten if available. Third, because the most nutritious foods are often available only seasonally when certain trees are in fruit, macaws need to travel extensively to find them.

Sleeping

Most macaw species sleep or roost communally, from dusk until it becomes light enough to fly the following morning. Communal roosting not only reduces the threat from potential predators by the increased collective awareness, but also helps in the communal interaction of pairs.

Behavior and Social Systems

The behavior of macaws in the wild is not very different from that of adult birds bred in captivity. Nevertheless, because wild birds congregate in large numbers and can act as a flock, rather than only as a pair, some aspects of their behavior can be extended and exaggerated in the wild. Hand-reared pet birds kept on their own will of course show little or no social behavior unless they are paired off for breeding in later life.

Flocking

In the wild, most macaw species are gregarious and live in small groups or flocks. Birds within the group will pair and form strong bonds; these pairs, however, no matter how strong the pairing may be,

◀ A pair of scarlet macaws *(Ara macao)*. Birds kept in outdoor aviaries can be housed in a variety of different barrels or house boxes such as this one used at Birdworld. Access to the entrance hole should always be easy to reach from the perching provided.

will for much of the time still live with other macaws in a group. The advantages of flocking behavior are obvious: Macaws living as a group have a much better chance of seeing danger approaching and so can increase their chances of survival. Living within a group provides unpaired macaws with more choices when selecting new mates. In addition, once a pair has bonded, the interactions between the pair and the other group members help to strengthen the pairing still further. Being a member of a group also helps individual birds because the flock is more successful in locating new food supplies.

Although macaws prefer to live in groups the bonds among group members are not strong. It is common for pairs of macaws to leave one group and join another; they may even travel on their own for at time before encountering others of their own species.

Pairing

The basic pairing process does not differ greatly between wild macaws and those bred in captivity, other than by the obvious fact that wild macaws have more potential partners from which to choose their future mates, or for later re-pairing to a new mate. In most cases, mate selection is initiated by the female, which shows submission to a male and pulls at his lower mandible—a gesture intended to encourage him to feed her. After pairing has been initiated, the male will then become the dominant bird in promoting pairing behavior that ranges from preening and feeding to copulation, which in a strong pairing can take place almost daily.

Preening

Preening takes place within established pairs but also more widely among all the macaws in a group. Preening not only is a social interaction that provides reassurance to the birds but is also essential to feather care and maintenance. Thus, any two birds may preen each other regardless of their relationship within the group.

Preening is important to all macaws to keep their feathers in good condition. It can be done by the bird itself, a mate, or other group member.

Bathing and Showering

Most macaws in the wild and in captivity love bathing in shallow water during hot weather. Rain showers are greatly enjoyed, too, with the birds outstretching their wings and even hanging upside down to make the most of the rain. A bath is usually followed by prolonged preening—which can entail self-preening as well as group members preening each other.

Breeding

Wild macaws will generally breed and rear young once or on occasion twice each year. Average numbers of eggs and incubation and rearing times, where known, are individually described later in the Macaw Species section. A nesting site favored by most species is a freshly hollowed crevice in a tree, particularly in a palm if available. Some macaws have other preferences, for example the red-fronted macaw that breeds and rears young on cliff shelves, a practice not common in other species. Young macaws generally fledge and become independent quicker in the wild than is usually the case in captivity; this characteristic is almost certainly due to necessity. Each year, macaws breed and try to rear their young when food supplies, particularly fruiting trees, are at their most abundant; therefore, it is essential that first clutches be fledged well before the available food supply starts to diminish. This allows the birds time to incubate and rear a second brood when the first clutch has failed. Fledging while food is abundant also helps the young macaws as they must compete with other more experienced adult macaws for the available food. It is then not surprising that chicks hatched late do not fare as well as those hatched earlier in the year.

Macaws as Pets

The suitability of keeping macaws as pets in most cases depends on whether the prospective owner of such a bird really does have the time, space, and financial resources required to provide for all of the bird's needs. As stated throughout the text, only hand-reared birds should be considered as house pets; wild-caught birds, even if still available, rarely adapt to such a life style sufficiently so that they can be considered happy.

Important Considerations Before Buying

Having come to a decision to go ahead and obtain a young macaw, several considerations and some preparation should be undertaken well before the day when you actually receive the new bird you have decided to buy.

Housing

The cage or aviary that the macaw will live in should be ready and waiting before the bird arrives home. Young macaws probably will not have experienced many such dramatic changes in their environment; readiness is, therefore, important because it allows the macaw to settle as quickly as possible in its new home.

Diet

It is not uncommon for young macaws that have recently been moved to new and different surroundings to become nervous and reluctant to eat. For this reason, the bird's diet should be planned in advance so the food can be bought and prepared prior to the macaw's arrival in the house. When first placing the bird in its new cage, food dishes should already be available within the cage. Ordinarily, these dishes are placed on one side of the cage, close to and level with the main perch, so that when perched the new macaw is always close to available food. The correct diet plan for the macaw—at least for the first few days when the new bird will undoubtedly be nervous and probably unwilling to experiment with new foods—should consist of the same food or closely resemble the food it has been receiving from the breeder. Changing the diet, although perhaps advisable in the long term, should not be done until the young macaw has settled and is feeding well.

Time and Attention

On its arrival the new macaw should receive as much time and attention as its owners can possible lavish on it; this is particularly true during the first few weeks when the macaw is still settling in. In many cases, throughout the rearing and weaning process, hand-reared macaws are cared for predominantly by one person. The loss of this person and the complete change in its environment can make the macaw feel insecure; this, in turn, could adversely effect its appetite and eventually its health. If routinely there is no one present in the house during the day, serious consideration should be given to receiving the macaw during a holiday period or even to taking time off from work to give the bird the attention it will require during its first week in its new home.

Young hand-reared macaws need plenty of attention, particularly when they have been recently acquired and are in unfamiliar surroundings.

Noise

Macaws are among the noisiest of all house pets. If you plan to keep the macaw in a house or apartment where there are many neighbors living in close proximity, then you need to seriously question whether keeping such a potentially noisy pet is really possible.

Other Household Occupants

During the first few weeks after its arrival, other large domestic pets, such as dogs or cats, should be kept away from the macaw while it settles in and gains confidence. Young children also need to be supervised when they are near the macaw to keep them from making sudden noises or movements that might alarm the bird.

Choosing a Macaw

When choosing a macaw the first question to arise is what species of macaw to keep. To some extent, this is a matter of personal preference, although the choice will be limited to some degree by external factors, such as the species that are available as hand-reared birds; the varying costs of different species, the size of some species (which may restrict the viability of keeping the larger species); and last, the conservation status of certain species (an important consideration). Macaws that are endangered in the wild and that are not firmly established in captivity should not be kept individually as pets but instead should be paired up for breeding. The high price of such rare species, however, is usually enough to discourage most potential buyers from the house-pet market.

You have now considered the suitability of each species by its size as well as the facilities you have available. Then after deciding on the species you prefer and having found the appropriate breeder or dealer who has young captive-bred birds for sale, it is not a case of selecting one from the group or clutch of birds in front of you as your future pet. The first criteria is to look for any signs of good or

Different species of macaw vary greatly in size, color, and temperament. Serious consideration should be given as to which species can best adapt to the facilities the owner has to offer.

poor health. These signs are basically the same as for adult birds, which are described in the chapter Health Care. If the bird seems healthy, try to assess its health status: Look at the weight of the bird, particularly if the bird has been weaned only recently as many macaws prove difficult to wean. Examine any macaw you are considering to ensure that it has a good layer of fat covering the chest, which shows the bird was properly weaned. Otherwise, the macaw may already be weak and will prove difficult to feed. Check other obvious signs of good health, including the following: eyes that are bright and clear; breathing, strong and does not sound obstructed; nostrils, clear of discharge; body and wing feathers, in good condition and without bare or plucked areas; bill and toenails, in good condition and there are no obvious injuries elsewhere on the legs. Finally, check the bird's general

Macaws as Pets

appearance: Its posture should be erect, held firmly; also it should be alert.

If after your scrutiny several of the young macaws seem to be healthy and in good condition, you can then try to pick the bird that is most likely to make the best pet. This is not always easy to determine, but without doubt a confident macaw will settle and tame much better than a nervous macaw. When looking at a group of macaws, try to establish which of those birds remain alert and confident when being viewed and which try to hide or turn away. A macaw that will hold eye contact without appearing to panic is probably the best bird to choose, especially if it will follow the movements of its viewer while still holding eye contact. Likewise, when a hand is stretched out toward the cage, it is the bird showing indifference or interest that should be picked, rather than one that panics or shies away. Of course, these can only be considered rough guidelines as young macaws will not always behave as expected when faced by a group of strangers. Nevertheless, as long as the birds being viewed are hand-reared and are healthy few problems should be experienced in taming them, no matter which individual bird is chosen.

Acclimatization and Quarantine

Acclimatization relates to helping the birds adjust to a significant temperature change in the environment in which they are kept. Usually, this word is used in connection with birds that are imported from a tropical climate to a different climatic zone. Nevertheless, acclimatization is important when dealing with hand-reared birds. In rearing, these birds are generally kept in a very protected environment and as such may be very susceptible to drafts, cold, or excessive heat in their new home. Thus, care should be taken to ensure that the bird is comfortable and warm enough on its arrival in the house. Moreover, attempts to introduce young macaws into outdoor aviaries should only be undertaken with caution, particularly in regions where

the weather can be unpredictable. A gradual approach is always safe. You can start by putting them outdoors during the day and returning them inside, or placing them in a heated shelter, at night.

Quarantine of all new birds is a practice that should be undertaken routinely before introducing the new birds into any large, established collection of psittacines. This should be done not only to protect the birds already in the collection, which deserve the owners' foremost consideration, but also to facilitate close observation of the new bird for the purposes of monitoring its overall state of health and ensuring that it is eating its food (an incoming bird may merely throw its food on the floor without ever eating it). Of course, young macaws that are to be kept singly as pets do not need a period of quarantine. It is still wise, however, to keep the new macaw under close scrutiny for the first few weeks not only to check its health and whether it is adjusting to its new diet, but also to ensure that the bird is comfortable in its new environment.

Handling and Restraint

Macaws are among the largest and most potentially dangerous psittacines for an inexperienced handler to restrain. A bite from even one of the small macaw species can be extremely painful; the large species such as the hyacinthine is easily capable of removing one or several digits from the handler's hand or inflicting severe lacerations to his or her arm. For this reason direct restraint of large macaws should be kept to a minimum. However, restraining the bird will be necessary when undertaking routine health care—such as worming, feather clipping, toenail trimming—or checking on the health of a bird that appears to be unwell.

All but the most experienced handlers are advised to always wear gloves when handling large macaws. This will greatly reduce the damage inflicted to a handler's hands which are the most vulnerable areas to macaw bites. Macaws are most

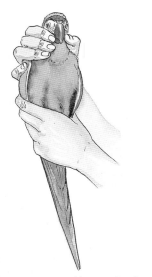

When holding a macaw, position one hand around the back of the bird's head, thereby securing either side of the lower mandible. With the other hand, secure the wings and legs.

easily caught once they are on the floor. You can cover the bird with either a net or a large towel and then carefully seize it. In holding a macaw, place the first hand around the back of the head with your thumb and index finger reaching around to the sides of the bird's lower mandible; next, with the second hand support the main part of the bird's weight holding the legs and wings at the same time to prevent the bird from struggling. Again, handling macaws can be dangerous; if you have any doubt, seek experienced assistance before attempting to handle your bird.

Transporting Macaws

Boxes that are intended for use in transporting large macaws need to be extremely sturdy to withstand the attentions of a macaw's bill. If the macaw is to remain inside the box for several hours on a long journey, carrying boxes can be made from strong wood. There are, however, a wide range of commercially produced dog and cat carrying boxes that will prove ideal for transporting macaws, as long as they are sturdy enough and a few alterations are made. First, if the macaw is going to remain in the carrying box for a long period of time, it will need something to perch on to prevent its feet from suffering cramps (which occurs if the bird is left to stand on a flat floor surface); a thick, sturdy perch should be fastened across the width of the box at about one third of the way up. Placing the perch at this height gives the bird sufficient head clearance space above, so the macaw can stand erect comfortably. Most domestic animal carrying boxes have a grille-type door or large ventilation holes on the side; the doors allow good ventilation but the large grille openings can be a disadvantage because they let too much light into the box. The higher light level tends to increase the macaw's awareness of what is happening around it, thus increasing the stress to the bird. This problem is easily solved by covering the carrying box with a thin cloth.

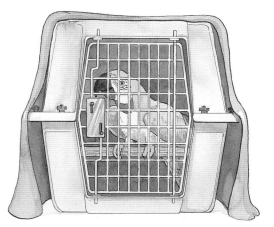

Macaws should only be transported in a strong, well-ventilated carrier. A cloth can be used to cover the carrier to reduce stress and avoid drafts during transit.

One final point to remember when transporting macaws is that large macaws should be housed individually while they are being moved. Otherwise, the limited space and the stress involved can lead the birds to fighting. Of course, food and water must be provided, particularly to young, recently weaned macaws if they are to remain in transit for several hours.

Bill and Toenail Trimming

As with all psittacines, the bill and toenails of a macaw are continuously growing throughout the bird's life. In the wild, macaws wear down their bills by scraping or gnawing on tree branches and their toenails are naturally worn down when rubbed against the wood in the course of their normal clambering activities. Captive macaws need to have their cages furnished with natural perching, such as apple branches, which must be replaced with fresh ones as often as possible. They also should have extra pieces of wood, small enough so the birds can hold them in their feet while they chew on them. Nevertheless, despite the presence of such wood, it may still prove necessary to trim either the bird's bill or its toenails. Such a procedure will require two people as the bird must be held firmly and safely before the trimming can be attempted. If you doubt your ability to carry this out, then ask an experienced person to help or take the bird to an avian veterinarian.

Trimming the bill of a macaw can be done quite easily by using commercially available clippers designed especially for this purpose. If you cannot obtain them in your area, there are other clippers available for use with dogs and cats that will work equally well. Remove as little as possible; the bird must be given the opportunity to do the rest itself by chewing. Also, be careful not to alter the shape of the bill. The last and most important precaution is to ensure at all times that the bird's tongue is clear of the clippers while the bill is being trimmed. Any injury to the tongue could well prove extremely

Chewing wood, provided either as fresh perching or in graspable chunks, can prevent the bill from becoming overgrown.

serious. Having removed the most overgrown areas of the mandible the bird should then be given as much available gnawing wood as possible. The wood will enable it to wear down the rough edges left by the trimming and to keep the bill from overgrowing again too soon.

Trimming the toenails of captive macaws is probably the more common of the two procedures that might have to be carried out periodically. Again, as little as possible should be removed at one time. Keep in mind that as the bird's toenails grow longer so do the veins that run inside them. Therefore, long-neglected toenails cannot be cut back too severely as care must be taken when trimming to safeguard the veins. Holding each toenail up against sunlight may allow you to see the vein. If this is not possible, toenail trimming should be done carefully, a little bit at a time. Between cuttings, provide the bird with natural branches for perching to give it the opportunity to wear down the toenails for itself. In cutting the toenails, always

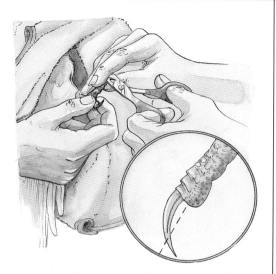

Trimming of the toe nails should always be done with care to avoid cutting into the quick.

hold the clippers at an angle to ensure that the upper surface is slightly longer than the lower surface of the nail. This angle conforms to the natural shape of the nail and helps the bird in wearing down the rough edges created by the trimming.

Feather Clipping

Feather clipping is an avian procedure that is carried out on the flight feathers of one wing, so that if a bird tries to fly it is imbalanced and cannot do so. In macaws and other psittacines this can be done for a number of reasons. Macaws in public collections are often kept at liberty and living in a barrel or box that is surrounded by perching. This arrangement allows the birds to wander without caging or physical restraint. In such cases the macaws are nearly always feather clipped periodically to prevent them from flying away. Although, sometimes, if the macaws have been living there for several years and have bred in their barrel, they can

be left to feather up and fly at liberty and will seldom wander far away. Also, when young macaws are brought into a household environment and are extremely nervous and flighty, it can be advantageous to feather clip them; this way, when placed outside their cage or on a stand, they do not become a problem by repeatedly jumping from their perching and flying around the room, thus risking damage to themselves or to items that they might knock over.

When feather clipping a macaw, the bird must be restrained securely while one wing is held outstretched. Here, too, an assistant is required. The long flight feathers on a bird's wing are arranged in two rows: The ten outer feathers are the primaries, which are the most important to the bird's flight. The ten inner flight feathers are the secondaries. In feather clipping, generally the outer two or three primaries are left intact so that when the bird folds its wing the wing appears normal; cutting them spoils the appearance of the bird at rest. Only the inner seven primaries are trimmed, along with all of the secondaries. The feathers should be trimmed

An unclipped macaw that is let loose inside the house can cause serious damage to itself and to household objects.

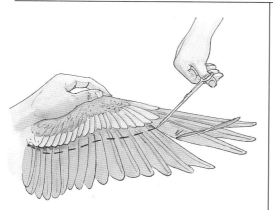

When feather clipping a bird, one hand holds the wing outstretched and feels where the wing bone ends. Cut the flight feathers below the level of the coverts with the other hand.

just below the level of the wing coverts which can be found about half way up the length of the flight feathers. Care should be taken when trimming to avoid cutting any young feathers (called *blood feathers*) that are growing through. As they are still growing, blood feathers have a living vein inside them that will bleed if it is cut.

Marking Macaws for Identification

Marking macaws for the purpose of identifying them is becoming increasingly important nowadays for two reasons: To deter bird thefts, and more important, as an aid in recordkeeping of captive-bred birds. After putting together a pair of macaws in a breeding cage, they can be extremely difficult to distinguish from each other if they have not been given identifying marks. Mistakes often result when unmarked birds are later paired to other birds; such macaws therefore may need to be retested to determine their sex. Various marking techniques can be used as an aid in identifying individual macaws. The most common are described as follows.

Close Banding

Close banding is becoming routine practice for all captive-bred parrots in most countries where they are being bred. The bands each have an individual number and a series of letters. These assignations help in keeping track of not only the bird's sex but also its blood lines, former owners, and previous mates. For additional ease in spotting the sex of a bird from outside an aviary holding a number of similar birds, close bands are normally put on different legs according to the bird's sex. Males are banded on the right leg; females, on the left. This last method is not used by all breeders but is commonly employed when trying to pair birds in a group.

Microchip Implants

The use of microchip implants is increasing as a result of the great number of bird thefts presently taking place. Any external marking, including close bands, can be removed with a little effort; the microchip, which can be injected into the bird inside a loose area of skin (commonly either in the neck or under the wing), was created to give each bird an individual number and other information that cannot be removed. The information contained within the chip can be picked up by a scanner passed over the bird's body. This technique is still new but is being used with apparent success.

Spray Marking

When a number of birds of the same species are placed together in a flight cage so they can select their own mates, spray marking, a short-term technique, is commonly used. To easily identify the birds at a glance without the need to catch them and examine their bands, a harmless colored spray can be used to paint the birds with variously shaped markings that can be seen from a distance. A confusion of fluttering birds always ensues when a breeder enters an aviary to transfer paired birds into their breeding cages; this marking method helps the breeders in catching and pairing each bird with its chosen mate.

Tail-feather Clipping

Also a short-term marking technique, tail-feather clipping is used when two similar birds are being temporarily housed together and need to be identified from each other. This can be easily done by clipping one or two of the central tail feathers of one of the birds, thus making one bird different from the other for a period of time until one or both birds moult.

Taming and Training

Once the macaw has settled into its new home and is eating well the owner can begin to work toward building a relationship with the bird. Macaws are highly intelligent animals and with time and patience the bird can not only become very tame and affectionate toward its keeper but can go on to mimic speech as well. With special training, some birds can do many other amusing things; trained parrots can be seen in shows all over the world doing anything from riding a bike to demonstrating feats of counting and even balancing objects. Such specialized training is beyond the scope of most owners; therefore, it is not described in detail here. This section concentrates on building and strengthening the relationship between the macaw and its owner and touches upon training the bird to mimic sounds, words, and even whole sentences.

Provided that you have obtained a young hand-reared macaw as your pet, it is likely the bird is already tame; it may also be nervous and disoriented by its new environment if recently purchased. In the early days after its arrival, the owner's time with the macaw must be spent reassuring the bird to slowly build up its confidence in its new owner and environment. After gaining confidence, the young macaw will be only too willing to seek the attention and affection of its new owner.

The first step in reassuring a young hand-reared macaw is to spend time sitting near it, thereby allowing the macaw to become used to seeing you and become familiar with the sound of your voice. Attempts to touch the bird should not be rushed if the bird still shows nervousness; the owner should wait until the bird is showing positive interest in establishing contact. At this early stage your sitting near the young macaw may make it slightly nervous; nevertheless, such birds are never kept isolated during the rearing period, so it is important to give them somebody they can relate to as soon at possible. This interaction with you will greatly speed up the time it takes for the bird to settle into its new environment. Shortly after the settling period the macaws should begin displaying a confident interest in your presence. You can encourage your bird to seek more contact with you by offering it food, which it will soon confidently and eagerly accept. At this stage your bird may allow you to touch it; try to pet it gently on its chest.

Once the bird is confident and interested in its new surroundings it can be allowed some degree of

When first venturing outside its cage in new surroundings, a macaw will appreciate a play perch—which need not be quite as elaborate as this one.

Macaws as Pets

freedom from the cage. At this stage, however, the bird should be feather clipped to prevent it from flying around the room and into objects because it could injure itself in the process. Leave open the door of the cage; you will soon find the bird climbing out and going to the top of its cage. If your macaw will be allowed to remain on the top of its cage for extended periods of time (with supervision, of course), a perch can be affixed to the top of the cage to make perching more comfortable. The bird should react confidently to this freedom and show a keen interest in the movements of its owners when they are in the room. Now that your macaw is readily accepting food from your fingers and letting you touch its chest, it can next be encouraged to step onto your arm.

Begin by offering your arm for the bird to perch on. The arm, rather than the hand, is offered because it is sturdier and may instill enough trust in the bird to encourage its climbing onto it. For the bird to actually step off its cage onto another object it needs to have a certain degree of trust in the

A macaw's confidence is always more easily won by offering food treats. This is especially true when dealing with a newly acquired bird.

firmness of the object on which it will place its weight. Place your arm horizontally in front of your macaw and slightly above the level of its feet; macaws will always prefer to step upward onto a new object. If your bird appears unwilling to climb onto your arm, push your arm gently against the bird's legs to encourage it to step upward. Macaws are known to test any new objects with their bills, and a new perch is no exception. Therefore, a move by your bird with its bill toward your arm is not necessarily an act of aggression or going to result in a bite. Should the bird start to test your arm with its bill, raise your free hand in front of the bird to distract it. If your macaw still appears reluctant to climb onto your arm, while keeping your arm still in front of it, try to entice it by offering a food treat that the bird can reach only by climbing onto your arm. A nervous bird may not respond to this right away, but given time and patience it will eventually learn to trust your arm and willingly climb onto it.

Macaws are not among the best speech mimics in the parrot family; that talent belongs to the Amazons and African grey parrots who can mimic not only words but also sounds across a wide range of pitches; for example, they can imitate a dog barking or a telephone ringing. Given time and patience, however, macaws can mimic words and can even put sentences together. In trying to teach your macaw to speak, keep in mind that the concentration time of young macaws is not great; short frequent lessons are therefore much more effective than sitting in front of the bird for an hour at a time. The macaw is at its most alert when it is first approached, but its attention starts to diminish after about five minutes. Giving your macaw a reward whenever you try to teach it will give the bird a sense of anticipation that will greatly increase the level of the bird's attention when you approach it.

The word *hello* is often the first word tried in teaching birds to mimic. Try it on your macaw. Say the word to your bird clearly and slowly; exaggerate the two syllables: "hell-O." Make your lessons about five-minutes long and reward your bird with food at the end. You can give your bird as many lessons a day as possible. After the bird has learned to mimic the first word you can add others to it in the same fashion. Using the first word learned is important as it will trigger the macaw into mimicking the new words along with it.

After the bird has become used to mimicking, further improvement may be facilitated by covering your bird's cage with a cloth to block its vision during training. Once deprived of the opportunity to see what is happening your bird will listen with much greater interest to hear what you are doing. This method helps the bird focus its attention and will result in its mimicking a greater number of the sounds it hears during such training periods. With persistence the range of words can be built up over many years. Some macaws have thus acquired an extremely large vocabulary.

Housing

Pet Macaws Inside the House

Hand-reared macaws are highly intelligent and when kept as pets can be extremely affectionate companions. On the other hand they also can be extremely destructive and noisy, so any decision to keep one as a pet should be carefully thought out. Selecting the most appropriate room within the house for the macaw to live in is perhaps the first consideration. The bird requires first a warm, draft free site that is not continually exposed to direct sunlight from a window. Placing the bird near a window may seem like a good idea, but it may prove to be a mistake. You may think that such a move will provide the macaw with something to watch when there is no one in the house. In reality this often leads to problems: The macaw can overheat if the window receives direct sunlight or become susceptible to colds or chills if the window has even the slightest of drafts.

Second, hand-reared birds seem happiest when they are placed at the center of activity and are constantly able to see things happening around them. Keep in mind, however, that although they enjoy being housed in busy, well-occupied rooms such birds may well become frustrated and noisy if they feel they are being neglected or ignored. Moreover, the noise created by the macaw can be bothersome not only to the owner but also to any neighbors that live nearby. The possibility of the noise provoking complaints from neighbors should be seriously considered; keeping a young macaw is a long-term commitment as that bird may well be living in your house for over fifty years. What may start out as minor irritations over noise can, over time, build up into major disputes.

The already mentioned potential destructiveness of macaws is another point that must not be underestimated. Hand-reared macaws are highly inquisitive and playful. As pets, their activities each day are wholly centered around playing with their owner and seizing the chance to wander outside their cage to find something new that interests them. Such excursions outside the cage, although of great importance to your bird's happiness, should always be supervised, otherwise its destructive interest in your household objects can have expensive consequences. Macaws are counted among the most powerful "chewers" in the parrot family. In the time it takes for the owner to leave the room and answer the telephone or make a cup of coffee a macaw at liberty can dismember a table, a chair, or anything else that may have drawn its attention.

On the other hand, the bird's well-being needs to be considered and attempts must be made to satisfy the macaw's curious and spirited nature. This is especially true when a bird is to live in a house that is empty for much of the day while everyone is at work. Such a macaw will of course need to be confined to a cage to prevent damage to the household furniture, but every effort should be made to provide the bird with things to do until the household's inhabitants return and can spend time with the bird. Provide your bird with food that has plenty of large nuts; give it other occupational foods, such as corn on the cob, that your macaw can enjoy biting or picking with its bill as it eats. The pieces of wood recommended earlier (see Bill and Toenail Trimming, p. 17) not only will keep your bird's bill and toenails trimmed to a suitable length but will stave off boredom as well.

You can try other things to occupy your lone macaw. Some people have even tried leaving a radio on near the cage. This has proved very successful and helpful in training the bird to mimic speech; apparently, it has an effect similar to that of covering the cage with a cloth (see Taming and Training, p. 20). Additionally, you can try to compensate by spending as much time as possible with the bird once you have returned home.

One last point needs to be mentioned that has particular relevance to the well-being of parrots that are to be kept as house pets. Whereas macaws kept in outdoor aviaries are able to shower in the rain or have available to them a large water area to bathe in, birds that are kept inside the house are

Housing

Spraying macaws that are kept in indoor cages with lukewarm water is important for keeping the feathers in good condition.

deprived of these benefits. For this reason, particularly during the hot, dry, summer months, be sure to provide your macaw with bathing water on a regular basis. Alternatively, spray the bird with a mister. Access to water is very important because when a bird is hot and sticky it resorts to excessive preening, which may leave its feathers too dry and without natural oils. Such plumage problems must be avoided as once developed, they are very difficult to reverse.

After considering the bird's requirements and adverse tendencies you can now look at how to provide suitable accommodations for your macaw. This is a question that must be reviewed well in advance of your purchasing the bird because the appropriate housing for it must be fully in place prior to the bird's arrival.

Several types of housing are available for the macaw owner to choose from. These fall into three main categories: pet bird cages, outdoor aviaries, and suspended cages. Hand-reared birds that are to be kept as pets inside the house are generally accommodated in commercially available cages and stands. Macaws that are kept primarily for breeding

are housed in conventional outdoor aviaries (the most prevalent type of housing for captive birds) or large indoor suspended cages. Some kits for building aviaries and suspended cages are available for purchase, but in most cases it is easier and cheaper to construct your own.

Cages and Stands

When considering accommodations for a pet macaw, the question usually centers around which of two things to use, a cage or a parrot stand? The best answer, not surprisingly, is a combination of the two. The cage is the main unit for keeping the macaw inside the house since, as we have already mentioned, it would be foolish to allow such a destructive pet unlimited freedom at all times; not only must you protect your household articles but the safety of the macaw as well. The house is full of

Suitable cages for a macaw.

24

dangers to an inquisitive macaw: objects that can fall on top of it; places where the bird can become trapped; and worse—PVC pipes and live electric wires that the bird can be tempted to chew.

Most owners generally like to allow their macaw as much freedom as possible when there are people in the house who can keep an eye on it. It is not convenient, of course, for you to carry the macaw around the house all the time. If the cage door is left open, often the macaw will be content to climb out the door and up to the top of its cage where it can watch all that is going on around it. The top of the cage, however, is not always the most comfortable surface for the bird to perch on because of the size and spacing of the cage bars. The bird, therefore, may become restless and start wandering away from its cage. It is obvious then, why parrot stands are widely used within the home.

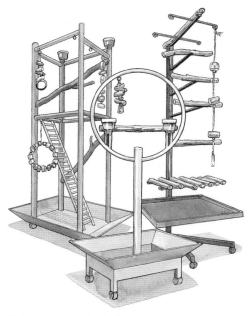

Various perches suitable for indoor use.

Moving your bird to a suitable stand after it has been let out of its cage allows it to perch comfortably for a number of hours. Moreover, the maneuverability of the stand allows you to position your bird wherever the family is concentrated, thus making your bird a part of the household's activities without the need to carry it continually or worry about damage to your furniture if the bird is wandering about on its own.

As discussed earlier, it is better if the perches within the cage are made from freshly cut branches. These will provide the rough texture your bird needs for a better grip; their diverse width and size also will help prevent cramps, which the bird can suffer on its feet if all the perching provided is of uniform size and shape and is not the right size.

Indoor Flights

Indoor flight, or aviary, is a name given to large cages that are constructed inside the house. These generally are used by those interested in providing as large an indoor cage as possible and who have the space and money to do so.

The advantages of an indoor flight are clear: It provides the bird with ample room for flying and exercising; it allows considerably more perches and other objects for the bird to chew or use for its own amusement. Its drawbacks, other than the obvious problems of having limited space and money to build it in the first place, are few. Indoor flights, if they are to be the macaws sole accommodation, should be well lit and well ventilated; also, they need to be cleaned regularly and thoroughly to avoid attracting household vermin that are looking for food.

Outdoor Aviaries

In purchasing or building an aviary for macaws, as with all parrots, the first consideration is that it should be constructed with materials that time has proved stand up to both the natural elements and

Housing

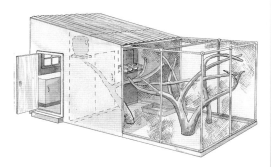

An outdoor aviary with a sheltered area and an open flight.

the powerful bills of macaws. Most aviaries used in aviculture are based on a wooden frame, but this is unsuitable for macaws because they would soon chew and destroy all the exposed wood accessible to them. Macaw aviaries usually have a framework constructed with either brick or metal.

Next you need to select the size of the wire mesh needed to cover the aviary. Although this is a matter of personal preference, with such large psittacines as macaws large-sized wire netting can be used because it is visually more attractive than smaller sizes. However, in my view, other than to keep the main cage inhabitants in, part of the reason for using wire mesh is to prevent native birds from entering and possibly contaminating the aviary. I recommend using small-size wire mesh or sometimes using both. Regardless of size, be sure the wire used is of a thickness and strength that can withstand the destructive bills of your birds over a long period of time. To make the aviary more attractive to look into, I always prefer the use of galvanized black wire mesh to cover the front and sides of the aviary. The black color of the mesh has a dramatic effect on the general appearance of the aviary. Additionally, it improves visibility and is helpful in obtaining better pictures when the birds are photographed through the wire.

The positioning of the aviary depends to a great extent on the size and shape of the land that the aviary is going to be built upon. I have always liked aviaries to have at least one section facing south to give the birds full advantage of the sun throughout the day, particularly in cool climates where the first warm rays of the sun are eagerly appreciated each day by the waking birds.

Your aviary construction must by design provide the macaws with shelter against the excesses of sun, rain, and particularly wind. To accommodate this feature, the back wall of the aviary should be solid and the back 7 feet (2 m) of the roof and sides of the aviary need to be covered.

Additionally, you must take every possible step to prevent rodents and other vermin from digging into the aviary. This can be achieved by excavating a layer of the floor within the aviary structure and covering this floor area either with concrete (with drainage provided by side holes that must also be blocked by wire mesh) or with wire mesh. In the latter case, an additional layer of floor medium will be required. Although a matter of preference, the two most commonly used floor mediums are sand and gravel. Both have their merits; nevertheless, sand is perhaps the most popular because it is quicker and easier to clean and maintain and thus leads to less disturbance of the aviary, particularly during breeding season.

After the main construction of your aviary has been completed, you must next think about the placement of internal furnishings, that is the nest box, food and water dishes, and perches.

Because in most cases the back of the aviary is sheltered, this is the most advantageous site for a nest box or nest barrel. Place the box high up in the back corner with the entrance hole looking out across the aviary, rather than facing forward.

Top left: Young blue and gold macaws *(Ara ararauna)* ▶ being hand reared.
Top right: An adult blue and gold macaw.
Bottom: A pair of blue and gold macaws. The female will usually initiate pairing behavior by encouraging her mate to feed her.

Housing

The sheltered area of the aviary is also the most suitable site for the food and water dishes. Food that is left out in the open can become waterlogged in the rain or dry in the hot sun. Additionally, to prevent disease in your macaws, food must be protected from contamination by the excretions of native birds that may roost above the aviary. Food dishes can be safely placed toward the back of the aviary on a shelf that has a raised lip along its edges to prevent the dishes from being knocked off by the birds. Or the dishes can be secured in place by means of metal frames. Your macaws will need water for drinking and, during hot weather, also for bathing. Locate the water containers in a protected and easily accessible site because they require daily cleaning and replenishment. Water that is allowed to stand for too long in warm weather can become stale or even be contaminated by native vermin.

Perching for the aviary is generally considered last but is one of the more important furnishings in an aviary. If the aviary inhabitants are to have easy access to food and water supplies as well as nest boxes, the placement of these elements must be decided first and later taken into account when the perching is being arranged. The type of wood used for perches greatly depends on what is available, but hard woods are always better because any soft wood perching is unlikely to remain intact and in position for very long once the macaws start to chew it. If available, apple tree branches make the best perches, particularly for indoor cages, as apple wood is a great aid in keeping the birds' toenails and bills trim.

The security of your macaws is one final point that bears consideration if you are to keep them in an outdoor aviary. As already mentioned earlier,

Aviary food dishes should be placed on a shelf with a protective barrier. Access is through a hinged door that is fastened when not in use.

macaws are an attractive target for theft. Picking a secure site for your aviary is the best start. Macaws are generally loud birds and more so when disturbed by intruders; if the aviary is located near your house, their cries can alert anyone in the house, especially if they come at an unusual time of the night when the birds should be roosting. Additionally, although aviaries can never be completely theft-proof, the use of strong wire mesh and padlocks can be helpful. Physical restraints at least make it difficult for any potential thieves to enter the aviary and can delay them long enough for someone in the house to become aware of the noise.

Indoor Suspended Cages

The growing use of suspended cages for keeping and breeding captive macaws has proved successful in recent years, although the size of cage needed to adequately house a pair of large macaws is much larger than that of most commercially available cages. Suspended cages basically have an all-wire construction. As their name implies, they are suspended above the floor to leave the area

◀ Top left: A military macaw *(Ara militaris)*.
Top right: A red fronted macaw *(Ara rubrogenys)*.
Bottom: A severe macaw *(Ara severa)* being encouraged to step onto its owners hand.

Housing

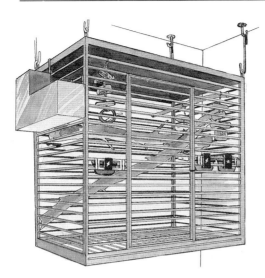

A suspended cage for a macaw.

underneath the cage clear for easy cleaning; the bottom panels of the cage are also made of wire to allow excess food and feces to fall through to the floor and out of the macaws' reach to eliminate the health risks that feces and spoiled food represent to them.

Securing your birds' food dishes in place is especially important in this type of cage because if these containers are allowed to overturn all the food will pass out of the cage. Revolving food trays, however, are now widely available for use with these cages. A unique advantage of using these trays is that they allow replenishment of the food and water supply without the need to actually enter the cage itself. Free of this disturbance, the birds seem to gain an increased sense of security soon after they become accustomed to their new accommodation.

As with any type of accommodation, an important point to remember in locating the suspended cage is that macaws are at their happiest when they are perching high above the heads of their keepers

and looking down on them. Suspending the cage with its base approximately 5 feet (1.5 m) above the ground will therefore allow you enough room underneath the cage for easy cleaning and maintenance as well as give your macaw the high perch it prefers, provided, of course, that the cage is of appropriate size.

The size of the suspended cage is determined by the size and species of macaw that is to be housed within it. For most of the large species the minimum dimensions required are 13 feet (4 m) in length by 6½ feet (2 m) in both width and height. Smaller macaws, such as the severe, noble, or yellow-collared need a cage 10 feet (3 m) long by 5 feet (1.5 m) wide by 6½ feet (2 m) high (the same height is necessary to also give the smaller macaws a high perch).

Perching should be provided across the width and at about half-way up of the suspended cage in at least three places (one of which must be within easy access to food and water dishes). This arrangement should provide the bird with sufficient perches and also leave it enough open space to jump or fly from perch to perch. For toenail and bill maintenance, perching can be supplemented with extra pieces of wood that can be either placed on the floor of the cage or attached to its sides.

Nest boxes for suspended cages are usually placed outside the cage and a hole is cut in the cage wires to provide access to the box. An inspection flap can be added to one side of the nest box to permit examination of nest contents without the need to enter the cage itself and disrupt the birds.

It is always best to place the nest box toward the back of the aviary where it will be least disturbed. Some people have experimented with L-shaped cages which are positioned with the L bend at the back of the aviary; they have found great success by blocking off the sides of the bend and locating the nest box in this area. Again, the increased security that this site seems to give the birds is generally reflected in the improved breeding results. Additionally, the L bend gives the birds a place to retreat out of sight without their having to use the nest box itself for this purpose.

There are therefore many advantages to using suspended cages for breeding macaws. Keep in mind, however, that this type of cage is intended for breeding birds and is not considered suitable for pet birds. The purpose of a suspended cage is to create a secure and undisturbed environment to make breeding birds more confident. But such an environment would deprive hand-reared pet birds of the human contact and attention they actively seek. A pet bird housed in this type of cage needs to be provided with a mate to which it can devote its time and attention.

Diet

Providing a captive macaws with an appropriate diet is of great importance. Food fulfills not only your bird's nutritional requirements but its occupational needs as well. When a varied and well-prepared diet is offered, mealtime can prove to be the highlight of the bird's day. Macaws are more omnivorous than most other parrots and will readily try a new food that is offered; they have a well-developed sense of taste, and it cannot be denied that they do derive great pleasure from eating their favorite foods.

Food, of course, should be prepared fresh each day. Be sure to purchase your bird's fruit and dry foods, such as seeds and nuts, from responsible suppliers who know how to properly handle and store their stock prior to its sale.

When feeding macaws it must be remembered that they are large, strong birds and any lightweight or unsecured food dishes that are offered to them are likely to be quickly tossed around and thrown to the floor. There are many different types of dishes and ways of securing them, so some experimentation will be needed to find the ones best suited to each individual bird. To compare two of the feeding arrangements previously mentioned (see Outdoor Aviaries, p. 25), a feeding shelf with a raised lip can prevent the food dish from sliding off but cannot stop the macaw from picking up the dish and tossing it off the shelf, as some are inclined to do. The commercially available food and water dishes that are secured by a metal holding frame, on the other hand, are perhaps the only real way to ensure that the food stays in place.

The quantity of food given to the bird daily must be moderated for two reasons. Hand-reared birds tend to be wasteful; when eating they throw much of their food out of the dish and onto the floor. Also, young birds can rapidly gain excessive weight that could eventually lead to health problems. The exact amount of food that should be provided daily depends on the species of macaw in question and the composition of the food being offered. Generally, I find that even the large macaw species live well on

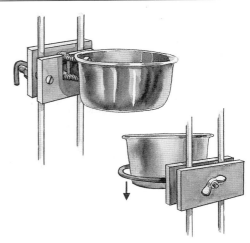

Food and water dishes are best secured to the sides of the cage.

about a cup of parrot mix (described subsequently) and a handful of assorted large nuts; the small species require even less. To assess how much fat your macaw is carrying you need to feel the bird's chest and ribs: There should be a reasonable layer of fat covering the ribs so that they cannot be individually felt, although the fat must not make the chest feel rounded. If the bird's ribs can be easily felt and the central breast bone sticks out noticeably, the macaw is underweight and should receive increased food and also be wormed as a precaution; when a bird is still thin despite its receiving more food the advice of a veterinarian must be sought. On the other hand, if the bird's chest is very rounded and firm, the bird is probably receiving too much food and is overweight. This is an indication that the food supply may have to be decreased.

A Balanced Diet

At Birdworld Bird Park in Farnham, United Kingdom, where the author works, a diverse group of psittacines—ranging from large macaws to grass parakeets—are kept and bred on public display. To accommodate such a large and varied parrot collection, a mix, which is made up fresh each morning, has been developed that forms the basis for the diet of most of the psittacines, although various seeds, nuts, and other items are added to the dishes of some species according to their individual needs. For many of the macaws, particularly the large species, extra large assorted nuts are added to the main mix, which is made up approximately as follows.

Dry foods, consisting of peanuts, pine nuts, and a small amount of sunflower seeds, are put in a large mixing tub. To this is added freshly cut fruits—at least three different types are used daily—and freshly shredded cabbage. Boiled rice (prepared the night before and refrigerated) is rinsed, separated, and added to the mix. Next, assorted beans are thoroughly rinsed and blended in. Bread that has been broken into pieces and soaked in warm water sweetened with honey is also put into the mix. Finally, a multivitamin powder and oystershell or mineralized grit is added before the ingredients are thoroughly mixed together and dispensed to the food dishes.

Because this food mixture contains many moist items—such as cooked rice, soaked bread, and fruit—it provides a very good medium that the multivitamin powder and oystershell grit can stick to, thereby leading to a more effective take-up rate of these vitamins and grit in the diet. It should be noted, however, that if the mix is in direct sunlight in hot weather it can dry out after a few hours and may need to be replenished with a second afternoon feeding. Also, the food dish should be sheltered from the rain if possible, otherwise the food will become waterlogged and will separate.

Seeds and Nuts

As stated before, peanuts, pine nuts, and to a lesser extent sunflower seeds are a part of the main food mixture that most psittacines receive daily. In the case of the large macaw species, their diet

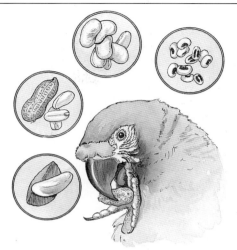

Macaws should receive various seeds, nuts, beans, and lentils daily.

consists of about two-thirds parrot mix and one-third large mixed nuts (Brazil nuts, walnuts, and hazelnuts, for example) as well as small nuts, all of which should be widely available in most countries where aviculture is practiced. Coconut is greatly enjoyed by the large macaw species and can be fed as a treat.

Small macaw species are not given large nuts, such as Brazil nuts, but still receive an increased amount of seeds and small nuts with the standard parrot mix.

If you are unable to make your own fresh parrot mix each day and you are using a dry seed mix based predominantly around sunflower seed, it is then important that you obtain a high-quality sunflower seed which has a larger kernel and lower oil content than the less expensive seed. Again, as with all foods, sunflower seed should only be obtained from a reliable seed dealer to ensure that the seed has been cleaned thoroughly and packed properly. It is bad economy to buy from an inexpensive source as the risks of disease from dirty seed are high.

Diet

In addition to the legumes and grains (discussed next) provided as part of the mixture, young, recently weaned macaws eagerly welcome an offering of sunflower sprouts. To encourage the seed to sprout, soak it prior to feeding the bird.

Legumes and Grains

Legumes are widely used in the feeding of captive psittacines because when allowed to sprout they can be an exceptional source of protein, amino acids, and vitamins. The preparation and combination of different legumes vary among different bird keepers, but the most widely used and most readily available varieties include soybeans, chickpeas, black-eyed beans, mung beans, and lentils. Regularly preparing and adding a mixture of these legumes to the normal seed based parrot diet will greatly improve its nutritional value when it is not possible for you to make your own mix as described earlier. Grains, including corn and barley, may be handled in a similar manner.

Always store legumes and grains dry. For use, they must be prepared two days in advance of feeding. For the first 24 hours keep them completely submerged in water so that they can absorb as much moisture as they will need to begin sprouting. On the second day, rinse thoroughly and place them in a tray with a moist cloth across the bottom; for the second 24 hours they should remain continually damp (the cloth in the bottom of the tray will help), but they also need air to sprout.

Before using them, it is important that you thoroughly rinse the sprouts in a sieve; during the soaking step the water surrounding them will begin to ferment and the bacteria thus formed could prove toxic to the birds if the sprouts are fed to them without rinsing.

Fruits and Vegetables

Macaws, unlike the Amazon and other South American parrots, generally receive a diet princi-

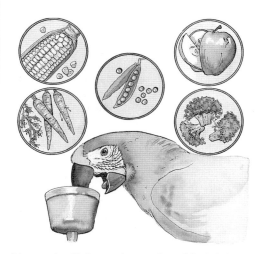

Macaws should also receive a variety of fresh fruit and vegetables every day. The selection should be from changed time to time to stimulate interest.

pally based on seeds and nuts, but for proper nutrition they also must regularly eat a variety of fruits and vegetables. With macaws, the most popular fruits appear to be apple, pear, orange, grapes, apricot, papaya, and banana. Not all should be fed as this would prove extremely wasteful. Give your macaw at least two of these fruits daily, however, and vary them from time to time to add interest to the diet.

Fresh vegetables must also be given to the bird daily but in limited quantity. The following are among the most nutritious: pea pods, baked potato, cabbage, green beans, cucumber, and (by far the favorite of most captive macaws) corn on the cob.

Other Foods

The other foods that help in feeding macaws a balanced diet include the following items:

Bread: If the birds can be persuaded to eat it, bread is an excellent addition to their diet. Soaking the bread in a diluted honey solution proves popu-

34

lar with the macaws; honey should not be added too liberally, however; it must be used in moderation.

Boiled Rice: Rice must be boiled, cooled, and rinsed, as previously described. Aside from providing an excellent medium for administering vitamin and mineral powders, rice adds fiber to the diet.

Grit: Macaws should be offered grit throughout the year to aid in their digestion. There are two main types: (1) mineralized grit, which should be regularly fed to pet macaws but fed to breeding birds only during winter; and (2) oystershell grit, which is high in calcium and should be fed to breeding birds during the spring and summer.

Animal Protein: Macaws in the wild will consume animal protein should a carcass be available. They have also been observed actually catching lizards and even small mammals, although more frequently so when rearing their young. Captive birds that are regularly fed sprouting legumes are probably receiving sufficient protein; nevertheless, when they are occasionally offered meat they relish it. Meats cooked in oil or fat should be avoided, but lean, cooked meat and poultry make a welcome treat.

Vitamins and Minerals

No diet can ever be perfect for captive macaws. For this reason, your bird's food mix should be supplemented daily with vitamin and mineral powders. Several such products designed for use with domestic animals have been available for many years and are useful for psittacines. In recent years, however, some products specifically developed for psittacines have proved highly successful. I have found three particular products to be extremely helpful: The first is a balancer that is added to the food on a daily basis; the other two were developed to deal with specific situations.

Vitamin and mineral supplement for birds (8 in 1) is added to the food daily and provides all the vitamins and minerals needed for a balanced diet when fed in conjunction with a sound, varied parrot diet.

Vita-Flight vitamins (Mardel) is a palatable, multipurpose, water soluble, high-potency product. It has especially high concentrations of vitamins A, C, and E. These three vitamins are rapidly used up by a macaw during times of stress, ill health, or molting. Therefore, this product is given to birds that do not appear to be in full health, birds that have recently been moved or have undergone a change in food, or birds that are approaching the molt. It should be noted that many macaws, particularly those receiving a predominantly seed-based diet, can be found to be deficient in vitamin A.

Avimin (Lambert Kay) is a liquid mineral supplement for birds that is especially high in calcium and, as such, extremely useful to macaws during weaning; it is also recommended for any birds starting to show signs of calcium deficiency.

Health Care

Large psittacines, especially captive-bred individuals, are among the hardiest and most long lived of all the different types of birds. Pet macaws in particular, if they have been hand reared and kept individually, develop their own distinct personalities and can form strong bonds with their owners; this kinship usually gives the owner a good understanding of the bird's behavior. If you notice a change in your bird's habits for which no external explanation can be found, look more closely; odd behavior may well signal the beginning of a health problem. The information in this chapter, however, is only an introductory guide to the health care of macaws. If a serious problem is suspected, expert help should be sought immediately.

Routine Health Care

Health care of your macaw does not begin when the bird becomes ill but is a daily concern that should be a part of your day-to-day bird maintenance. Most of the steps in the health care routine can be regarded as common sense, but some of the more obvious considerations are listed below and deserve to be taken into account even before the actual purchase of a pet macaw.

Stress: Stress is an unseen but common killer of wild animals (including birds) in captivity. Even though in most cases stress is not directly responsible for the death of a bird, its presence and the increased adrenalin and hormonal response it triggers within the bird's body can often weaken the physical condition of the bird, thereby reducing the effectiveness of its immune system and making it susceptible to any one of the many infections that can affect a bird.

Food Supply: Again, the food offered to macaws must be freshly prepared each day and should be of a balanced and varied composition. All food items used in the diet, particularly fruit, should be of high quality. A sprinkling of a good multivitamin product should be added. Food placed in an outside aviary must be protected from the elements

Careful cleaning of all food and water dishes should be considered routine health care for macaws.

and from contamination. Remember that native birds and rodents could drop feces on the food or eat it.

Water Supply: Water is generally provided to the birds in a water dish or shallow pool. It is essential that water containers be cleaned routinely and replenished with fresh water. Many birds will not drink water that has been standing for too long. Additionally, such an open water supply can easily be contaminated by native birds and rodents, creating a risk for avian tuberculosis and similar diseases.

Worming: All captive psittacines should be wormed at least twice a year, even when the presence of worms is not evident. It is also good practice to routinely worm young fledging birds as soon as they become independent; it is possible for young birds to become heavily infested as a result of being continually fed by their parents over a long period of time. The different types of parasitic worms that affect macaws are described later in this chapter.

Signs of Poor Health

Macaws when kept as pets usually develop highly individual but consistent behavior patterns. Excessive moodiness and other odd behavior can

Health Care

therefore be noticed fairly quickly and alert the owner that the bird may not be feeling completely well. Irritability and other moods, of course, can often be brought on by external factors: For example, during periods of hot weather the macaw's environment can become uncomfortable, especially if the bird does not have access to bathing water or is not cooled with a mist sprayer. Despondency in a bird that cannot be reasonably explained, however, deserves serious attention, especially when it is accompanied by poor appetite and listlessness.

The physical posture of the macaw can also reveal possible signs of poor health. When a bird is healthy it is alert and holds its head high watching all that is happening around it. Generally, a less firm than normal body posture with the head and wings drooped and the abdomen sagging over the feet can be a sign of illness. A sick bird will also be less than alert and seem uncomfortable and unsure of its footing; often it can be observed shifting its weight from one foot to the other. Unexplained bulges in the bird's normally smooth body feathering may conceal an abscess or cyst, which may result from old injuries that have become infected. Remember that birds may feel threatened if observed from a close distance and may mask indications of poor health by appearing more alert than when they are relaxed. Therefore, when assessing a bird the initial observations should be made from a reasonable distance. Only after the keeper has gained an accurate idea of the macaw's body posture can the bird be approached to look for other indications of poor health.

The macaw's eyes can show signs of possible eye infections and give an indication of general poor health as well. The eyes of a healthy bird are fully open and watchful. Illness can cause the macaw to be less observant and to partially close its eyes. Often, there can be swelling on the upper or lower eyelids and the eyes may appear watery; these are mainly indications of an infection.

Breath sounds can also be a valuable guide to the macaw's state of health. Of course, when a bird

A sick macaw may have poor feathering, drooping wings, sleepy eyes, and will sit down upon its legs when perching.

is inspected from a very close distance, its breathing will become rapid; this is not a bad sign but merely the bird's natural fight-or-flight response taking effect. By listening to the bird's breathing closely, several indications can often be gleaned: Although rapid, the breathing should not sound forced as this would indicate an obstruction within the chest or windpipe; likewise, rasping or other similar noises in the breathing can be a sign of loose patches of dead tissue as can result with aspergillosis or similar conditions.

Finally, other areas that should be checked if ill health is suspected in the macaw include looking at the vent to ensure that it has not become clogged with defecation and that the feathers surrounding it are not stained, which may indicate enteritis. If the bird is to be caught for a physical examination, the chest can then be gently felt for signs of under- or overweight. The mouth, as with all psittacines, proves difficult to examine and any overzealous attempts to do so usually only lead to unacceptable levels of stress being inflicted on the bird, which may already be in a weakened state. Nevertheless, excessive amounts of saliva may be apparent even without direct examination of the bird's mouth; the macaw may appear uncomfortable and may repeatedly try to wipe its bill against the perches or other available objects.

Care of Ailing Birds

If the macaw is showing obvious signs of poor health it can be assumed that illness has taken a firm hold and treatment will probably be required. The sooner a sick bird is properly treated, the better. For this reason, steps must be taken prior to encountering any health problems with the bird to locate a veterinarian who is experienced in treating psittacines and whose practice is within a reasonable traveling distance.

Warmth is very important to an ailing bird; if the macaw is housed in an outside aviary, it should be caught and transferred indoors to a draft-free cage with a heat source maintaining a temperature

A hospital cage. Heat and security are of prime importance to sick macaws.

of about 86°F (30°C). The bird should have both food and water readily available within easy reaching distance of the perch it is sitting on. The placement of the food and water dishes within the cage may seem a trivial point, but in the case of a sick bird that does not feel compelled to eat or drink it is of great significance; if situated too far away, the bird might not make the small effort needed to reach the food and water.

Several types of commercial hospital cages are available, although few of them are large enough to accommodate macaws. Often a regular macaw cage situated in a draft-free room with a spotlight placed over the top of the cage will serve the same purpose. The important feature of a good hospital cage is that it provide a warm, draft-free, and secure environment, which will greatly reduce the amount of stress the sick bird is experiencing.

Preparation for the Veterinarian

When a serious health problem occurs and the assistance of an avian veterinarian is required, it would be helpful to the veterinarian if the macaw's owner could be ready to answer a series of questions relating to the bird's state of health and husbandry. Some of the most commonly asked questions are given below.
• How long have you owned the bird?
• Was it wild caught or captive bred?
• Is the bird housed on its own or with other birds?
• When were the first signs of poor health noted?
• Have any other birds that have been kept near-by shown similar problems?
• Has the bird recently been subjected to a change in its diet or water supply?
• Has the bird recently been moved to a new cage/aviary?
• Has it been introduced to a new mate or lost one recently?
• At any time in the past has the bird suffered a previous illness that you know of?
• If so, what treatment did it receive?

Aside from the information obtained through this standard inquiry, the veterinarian will need as much direct information as the owner can provide on the bird's specific illness from the time it was first noted. If a serious ailment is suspected, providing a fecal sample on the first visit to the veterinarian is helpful; the correct diagnosis can thus be rapidly obtained. This precaution will greatly increase the chances of successful treatment of the bird's ailment.

The trip to the veterinarian's office is a stressful event to the sick macaw. Therefore, every effort should be made to minimize its effects on the weakened bird. A dark carrying box is best because any daylight entering the box will increase the bird's awareness and anxiety will result. The box also needs to be well ventilated but draft free.

Common Macaw Illnesses

Ectoparasites (External Parasites)

Macaws can be affected by infestations of external parasites such as mites or lice, which live on the surface of the bird's skin and feed by burrowing into the skin. When infested, a bird shows signs of prolonged preening and scratching, general irritability, and in advanced cases bare patches of skin.

Treatment: There are many dusting powders and sprays available that can be easily purchased. Dust or spray the entire body surface of the bird, but take care to keep the powder away from its eyes, nostrils, and mouth. Also thoroughly clean the bird's cage and perches and dust or spray any areas of wood accessible to the bird that may still harbor parasites.

Endoparasites (Internal Parasites)

The most common internal parasites that affect macaws are tapeworm and roundworm. Birds that are kept in an outdoor aviary run a higher risk of infestation because the aviary can easily be contaminated by the feces of native birds or more directly by contamination of the macaw's food if small native birds can enter the aviary to feed from the food dish. There are no apparent signs of infestation, but examination of an infested bird's feces will usually confirm the presence of worms. Nevertheless, a heavy infestation will undoubtedly lead to a deterioration of the bird's general health. For this reason, preventive measures by routine worming are strongly recommended.

Treatment: Various brands of worming agents (Fenbendazole, for example) can be obtained from the bird's veterinarian. Give the medication to the bird directly in its mouth or by adding it to the bird's food or water over a period of several days. The use of such products, however, requires that an experienced veterinarian determine the correct dosage for each species to avoid mistakes.

Psittacosis (Parrot Fever or Chlamydiosis)

Although not a common illness in parrots, psittacosis is perhaps well known because it can affect humans as well. This condition is difficult to recognize because its signs are similar to those commonly associated with a host of other ailments. The most common symptoms are drowsiness, lack of appetite, weight loss, diarrhea, and sore or inflamed eyes.

Treatment: Psittacosis is a serious condition which can be fatal in macaws; if suspected, the advice of the bird's veterinarian should be immediately sought.

Coccidiosis

Coccidia are microscopic, protozoan parasites that can invade the intestinal tract. This organism can be a serious problem for macaws kept in outside aviaries as the most common form of contracting this condition is by the contamination of the bird's food and water by native birds or rodents. If the appropriate precautions are not observed in designing and constructing the aviaries (see Outdoor Aviaries, p. 25) and wire meshing with large openings is used, an infected native bird can easily enter and contaminate a series of aviaries. Signs of coccidiosis are intestinal bleeding, weight loss, and somewhat bloody droppings.

Treatment: Suspected cases of coccidiosis will require immediate attention from the macaw's veterinarian.

Respiratory Ailments

Problems in the respiratory system can be caused by bacterial, viral, or fungal infections. Generally, at the beginning it is difficult to distinguish one condition from the other because the symptoms are the same for all three types of infection. The most common respiratory condition is aspergillosis, a fungal illness that can often be found in freshly imported birds that have been subjected to poor housing and particularly overcrowding. For this reason, any wild-caught birds entering an established collection need to be closely examined, with special attention given to their breathing sounds. The beginning signs the various respiratory ailments share are forced breathing, wheezing, and nasal discharge; additionally, in fungal infections a clicking sound can be heard caused by patches of dead tissue moving in the air passages. General deterioration of the bird's health normally follows.

Treatment: Whatever the cause, respiratory ailments can be serious; at the first sign of any significant disturbance in the bird's breathing, veterinary advice must be obtained.

Pacheco's Disease

Among the most serious viral conditions that can affect any psittacine, but especially South American species such as the macaws, is Pacheco's disease. The virus responsible for this disease attacks with little warning and kills the affected birds with great speed.

Treatment: Once the virus is established, treatment is extremely difficult and is therefore based upon preventing the virus from entering the collection in the first place; strict quarantine of all newly imported South American psittacines is essential. A vaccine has been developed by Maine Biological Laboratories. It is administered by intramuscular injection.

Behavioral Problems

Macaws kept as pets can develop adverse behavior, often referred to as *stereotype behavioral problems*, which is a term used to describe habitual and exaggerated acts parrots resort to in times of stress and boredom. When stereotype behavior is allowed to develop, it can be highly distressing to both the bird and its owner because it can manifest in a number of unpleasant ways. One of the most common is surely feather plucking, but other reparative behavior can include repeated bouts of screeching and even self-mutilation. Because they are often encountered, a detailed discussion of each of these problems follows.

Feather plucking is perhaps the most widely seen problem. Birds usually start by pulling feathers from their breast or wings, but the plucking can

All types of toys and wood chews can be provided for a pet macaw to prevent it from becoming bored when alone.

escalate to the point where a bird is totally devoid of all feathering below the head.

New feathers are almost instantly removed by the bird as soon as they appear. A macaw in this condition is a pitiful sight.

Screeching can often occur in wild-caught birds whenever a stranger approaches. Hand-reared birds, however, screech to attract attention when the bird feels it is being neglected.

Self-mutilation is the most harmful of the possible stereotype behaviors, but is also the least frequently seen problem. The bird may begin chewing a certain part of its body, often the leg, wing, or skin underneath the wing. Over time the bird will continue to chew and scratch the affected part of its body, making it bleed. This can sometimes result in severe injuries and wound infection. Such cases should receive immediate specialist help.

Possible triggers for the onset of stereotype behavior could include a change in the bird's environment—a new owner or the presence of a new person or animal in the house—as well as a change in the bird's daily routine—such as a different feeding or play time. Hot weather can irritate the bird if it is denied access to water for bathing. Perhaps the most common cause is a sudden withdrawal or significant slackening of the daily attention a pet bird is used to receiving, which may be precipitated by a change in the family's routine or some other reason.

No definite treatment for stereotype behavioral problems exists other than supplying the bird with as much occupational therapy as possible. Macaws, as do all psittacines, love to chew and indeed require it to keep their bills and toenails down to their proper length. As a first step, regularly replacing the macaws perching and providing as much fresh chewing wood as possible may help in keeping the bird's mind off its adverse behavior. Birds that seem to be suffering from not receiving enough attention because their owners have to work often benefit from having a radio playing near their cage. Parrots seem to be fascinated by the radio noise, perhaps because there is no visual activity that can account for the sounds. Aside from these suggestions, the only other course of treatment is simply to spend as much time as possible playing with the macaw.

Breeding Macaws

Macaws kept in captivity can and do breed readily and successfully, provided their needs for mate selection, seclusion and security, diet, and appropriate nest sites are understood and accommodated. The need for successful captive breeding of macaws cannot be overstated: First, the presence of captive-bred birds acts to curtail the importation of birds from the wild. Second, strong, well-managed, self-sustaining captive populations can act as a genetic holding pool to help threatened wild populations of macaw species. For example, captive-bred birds can be released to strengthen falling wild populations or, more selectively, to add genetic diversity to small secluded populations that through inbreeding may be at risk for deterioration of important species characteristics.

It is hoped that the previous chapters have provided some understanding of the basic maintenance needs of macaws in captivity. Therefore, this chapter will look at the most important aspects of breeding in captivity, beginning with one of the most important: making sure that the two birds that are housed together are indeed a true pair.

Sexing Macaws

Throughout the history of aviculture macaws have been bred in captivity, often with proven pairs of birds going on to breed consistently for many years; however, if one is to consider the large numbers of macaws of different species that have been available throughout past aviculture, the level of breeding success has been extremely poor. Probably the main reason is that, as with most other monomorphic psittacines, in the past breeders had to guess in sexing their birds based on subtle physiological differences and observations of bird behavior and interactions. There can be no doubt that in many cases, even in recent times, many macaws of the same sex were mistakenly paired up for breeding. Fortunately, the advent of laparoscope examination to determine a bird's sex and more recently the technique of chromosomal sexing have

dramatically increased the chances for success in breeding captive macaws.

Sexing Birds by Physical Characteristics

Physical differences between male and female macaws of the same species do exist. In many mature birds the male has a slightly larger head. Its bill is also slightly more prominent, particularly at the base where along with the cere it can be noticeably wider. These differences, however, are difficult to recognize because their assessment is mainly a matter of comparison and interpretation. Moreover, the large-scale hand-rearing that exists today employs a wide range of diets that can result in significant size differences in adult birds of both sexes, making the slight size difference between genders that much more difficult to discern. Such subjective differences should never be completely relied upon, especially when at present laparoscopic and chromosomal sexing is so easily available.

Sexing Birds by Behavioral Characteristics

Observing the interactions of a group of macaws for courtship and pair-bonding behavior is very interesting, but is not a reliable way to sex birds. Mistakes can easily be made because if no suitable mate of the opposite gender is available, often two macaws of the same sex can form a pair bond and behave like a true pair, even to the extent of going through the mating motions. For this reason, macaws should always be sexed either by surgical or chromosomal techniques and then be close-banded or otherwise marked to prevent confusion. After marking, the birds' behavior can be studied to pick out the true pairs without the risk of mistakenly pairing up two birds of the same sex.

Laparoscopic Sexing

Laparoscopy is a surgical examination performed through a laparoscope. This instrument consists of a thin elongated probe that is about 6

Breeding Macaws

inches (15 cm) long and only 3 millimeters in diameter; a fiber optic cable runs through the center of this tube and transmits light from an attached source to facilitate viewing. An experienced operator inserts the probe into the bird's left abdominal air sac and through an eye piece situated at the other end of the probe is able to see the bird's sex organs and thus determine the correct sex of the bird. Certain individual birds can prove more difficult to examine, most commonly because of obesity; an excess of fatty tissue can obstruct the view of the sex organs. The main problems with this technique are the risks usually associated with any surgical operation, however simple; therefore, care should be taken to prevent undue stress to the bird before and after the operation, especially during catching

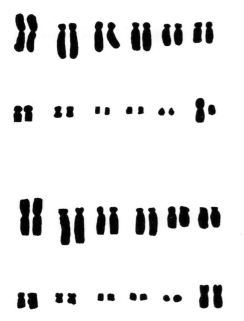

The chromosomes of the female and male macaw as seen under a microscope. The last pair in each group are the sex chromosomes, which are of unequal size in the female (above).

and later transporting the macaw to the place where the surgery is to be performed. It is normal practice not to feed the bird on the day of the operation as the digestive tract needs to be clear of food to prevent any possible complications.

Chromosomal Sexing

A laboratory test that uses the chromosomal differences in male and female birds to determine their sex is the newest technique available to the aviculturist. Most people regard it as the safest and best sexing method. Gathering the sample cells necessary to extract the chromosomes does not require stressing the bird with risky anesthesia and surgery. The sample can be obtained by gently pulling a growing feather (also called blood feather) from the bird, which is then sent to a laboratory where the pulp contained in the feather shaft is processed to perform the test. Chromosomal sexing is completely accurate, but it is essential to correctly label each sample and keep accurate records of the birds from which samples are taken. Otherwise, misidentification of birds can occur.

Record Keeping and Stock Management

Keeping good records of the birds in their care is a priority for all bird keepers, particularly for those keeping macaws species because these birds are extremely threatened in their wild state. As importation of many species from the wild slows down or stops, keeping track of the parentage of all macaws will be more important if the birds already present in this country are to form a long-term, self-sustaining captive population without the risk of inbreeding. This point gains significance when one considers that with the improvement of artificial incubation and neonatal care of hand-reared macaws it is already clear that a large percentage of all macaws currently being bred are the offspring of a relatively small percentage of highly productive breeding pairs. These prolific birds can produce three to four clutches a year because the first two broods are artificially reared. Although I am in no way suggesting that the breeding of such productive pairs should be limited, I do feel that there is a growing need to identify and make use of previously unproductive wild-caught macaws. These birds are largely unrelated to most of the breeding stock in the country and can therefore help the future genetic pool of the species to remain strong by preventing its becoming overdominated by the genetic material of the small percentage of highly productive pairs.

Additionally, keeping accurate records can be of direct help to macaw owners when they need to check back on routine bird maintenance matters such as worming, previous illnesses and treatment used, feather clipping, previous egg-laying behavior, changes in the bird's diet, accommodation of partner, and so on. The record card should also contain notes about anything unusual that may be observed in the bird's behavior, even slight signs such as poor appetite, listlessness, or poor body posture. As previously discussed, these could be the first visible signs of illness; your having an accurate, dated record of them can prove valuable to the veterinarian at a later date in making a diagnosis.

Pair Bonding

The advent of accurate sexing techniques for monomorphic species of birds such as macaws over the past decade has without doubt helped revolutionize the captive breeding of such birds. It is by no means enough, however, to merely house together a male and female of the same macaw species for them to breed. Because macaws are highly intelligent and sociable, when given the chance they spend much time indulging in social interaction with others of their own kind. Therefore, it is not surprising that the strong pair bonds developed by breeding pairs are not the result of random pairings but rather of individual bird pref-

erences. Macaws are highly individual in their behavior. They can exhibit a strong attraction as clearly as a strong dislike for another individual bird. For this reason, an arbitrary pairing of two macaws can run the risk of putting together two birds that, although of different gender, may dislike each other. Such an unsuitable pairing could prove intolerable to both birds and possibly distress them enough so that their health would suffer.

To avoid mistakes in pairing, macaws should be given every chance to select their own future mates. Prior to introducing a bird into a large aviary with other macaws of its own species for this purpose, however, the correct sex of the individual macaw must have been established. Also, the bird must bear a sex identification mark, such as a close band (in which case the identifying number is entered in the bird's record card) or any other distinctive marking painted on with a suitable agent. Then all that remains to be done is maintaining a close watch to ensure that the mate it selects is indeed of the correct gender and is appropriately unrelated.

Additionally, during the bonding process macaws also need to be closely observed for any signs of aggression. When several macaws are housed together for pairing, they are often competing for the same mate; serious fighting is then likely to break out. The risk can be minimized if pair bonding is carried out during the winter months, at least two to three months prior to the onset of the breeding season when the birds' hormone levels and competitive tendencies will be at their peak.

Top left: A severe macaw *(Ara severa)* playing with items ▶ on its play perching.
Top right: A clutch of young severe macaws being hand reared.
Bottom left: An adult yellow-collared macaw *(Ara auricollis)*.
Bottom right: A pair of yellow-collared macaws.

Breeding Macaws

Breeding Aviaries

The various types of housing for the accommodation of macaws have already been described in the chapter on housing. It may, however, be of some use to look more closely at some additional aspects of aviary preparation and care that apply during nesting time.

When incubating eggs or rearing their young the aviary must satisfy the birds' overwhelming need for seclusion and safety. It is common practice to cover the sides of the aviaries (the front is left open) when several pairs of macaws are being kept in adjoining sections to reduce the amount of interspecies aggression and resulting stress. If this is done, however, it is then important to consider how the keeper should approach the aviary. You must not walk straight down along the front because the birds, unable to see you coming, would suddenly be faced with having a possible aggressor appear right in front of them and be made to panic. When working with aviaries that have been covered, it is always better to approach them head on, by walking wide of them and then directly toward them. This way, the birds can watch you approach from some distance away and will not be suddenly startled.

Routine maintenance and cleaning of the aviary at this time must be done as briefly as possible to cause only minimal disturbance. Feeding, watering, and cleaning should all be done at the same time so that the birds will only be disrupted once a day; food that has fallen from the food dish must be removed each day, however, as this could lead to infection if fed to the chicks or could attract vermin into the aviary.

Nest Boxes

Many different nest box designs have been used to successfully breed macaws in captivity. Nevertheless, the most commonly used by far is the "grandfather clock" nest box which, as all psittacine nest boxes, should be about three times the macaw's own body length in height and one body length in width and depth. Other kinds of nest boxes include a horizontal version of the grandfather clock box, the barrel type box, and a whole assortment of differently shaped boxes, the most common of which are illustrated here.

It is clear therefore that there is not one universally correct type of box. To determine which type of box may best encourage the macaws' breeding attempts, it is probably of more use to examine more closely how well the different aspects of the designs will serve the macaws' nesting needs: Seclusion and the feeling of security within the nest box are of paramount importance. So, too, is the amount of daylight admitted inside the box. Nest boxes for macaw species need to be situated in the sheltered and more shady areas of the aviary to minimize light as much as possible. The shape and height of the box is important in keeping most of the sunlight entering the box through the entrance hole from reaching the hen as she sits on the eggs (most people prefer horizontal boxes for this reason). The size of the entrance hole is also of critical importance to nesting success. Ideally, the hole is only large enough for the adult macaws to be able to squeeze through. This way the macaws can easily guard the entrance when sitting inside the box and thus make the interior secure. A ladder consisting of wooden blocks secured to the interior of the front panel of the box is necessary to allow the adults and young birds to climb in and out of the box without difficulty. Additionally, the interior walls of the box need to have several blocks of wood secured to them in a random pattern that, without restricting the movements of the macaws within the box, will provide occupational chewing material for the hen

◀ An adult Illiger's macaw (Ara maracana).

47

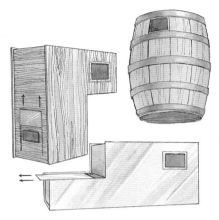

Various types of nest boxes that can be provided for macaws to breed in.

during the long incubation and rearing period; these chewing blocks also provide a target that helps in venting the frustration of the adult birds, which will often retreat into the nest box in a highly stressed state after the aviary has been entered for any reason. Another important detail, and one in which great differences exist among successful macaw breeders, concerns the medium needed to cover the base of the nest box. The most commonly used mediums consist of wood shavings or a half-and-half mixture of sawdust and peat. The preferred mix must be provided to a depth of 4 to 8 inches (10–20 cm); any unwanted excess is usually tossed out of the box by the macaws themselves.

Once the nest box is ready, the next decision concerns the site that will be the most suitable for placing the box within the aviary. As already explained, macaws undoubtedly prefer secluded, shaded areas for nest sites where protection from the elements and some direct sunlight are available. Wherever possible, the entrance hole to the box should be high above the keeper's head; remember that macaws derive a greater feeling of security from such a high placement. Moreover, I have always preferred nest boxes to be situated on a side

wall of the aviary, with the entrance hole looking out across the flight, rather than facing toward the front; the macaws will feel threatened if upon emerging from the entrance hole of the box they must look straight into the faces of people standing outside the aviary looking in. This point is of particular importance if the birds are being kept on public display or in a garden where children play during the summer months.

Most commercially manufactured nest boxes are equipped with an inspection flap that allows the interior of the box to be examined without the need to enter the box from the top by removing the lid. Nest box inspections should be kept at a minimum, especially in the case of macaws that are not yet consistent breeders. When the macaws are intended to rear their own young they should be allowed to incubate their eggs without the disturbance of nest box inspections. After seeing the first egg, unless something in the birds' behavior indicates that the eggs have been broken or discarded, the box should not be examined again until the day this egg is due to hatch; a brief inspection is appropriate at this time to ensure that the hen is not just sitting on eggs that are infertile or have ceased to develop.

At the end of the breeding season, unless the nest box provides the only shelter in the aviary and is a roosting place for the birds, the box should be completely emptied, cleaned, and stored in a dry place until the start of the next season. Prior to its return to the aviary, it is good practice to treat the exterior (but not the interior) of the box with a wood preservative; a treated box must be allowed time to dry, at least a week to ten days, before being placed in the aviary. It is, of course, essential that nontoxic preservative be used as macaws will often chew the box edges. As a matter of routine, nest boxes should also be dusted with louse powder before use.

Egg Laying

Most species of macaws lay their eggs in clutches of two or three eggs; occasionally the clutch may contain a fourth one. Nearly always, eggs are laid in the early to middle part of the morning. In the large species, a new egg follows every second day after the first one has been laid; in most of the small species, every third day. Incubation starts immediately after the first egg is laid; this means that the young will hatch at time intervals of two or three days, depending on the particular species, thus leading to a slight size difference in the chicks as they grow and develop. Nevertheless, this bears no significance as long as the available food is plentiful. The incubation period for most species of macaw is between 26 to 28 days. Individual incubation information is given in the species descriptions at the end of this book.

Special Care and Feeding of Parent Macaws

Once it is evident that the macaws have successfully hatched chicks the best approach is to leave the nest site completely undisturbed, unless the removal of one or all chicks is being considered with a view to encouraging a second clutch. Remember that aviary maintenance must be kept to a minimum at this time as parent macaws may not just be nervous but also highly aggressive toward their keeper. Provide plenty of fresh chewing wood to help relieve their anxiety.

Macaws need to have a ready supply of food while they are rearing young. Of course, the necessary precautions to protect the food dishes from the elements and contamination still apply; additionally, be sure to remove old and stale food from the aviary. Some types of food will be particularly welcome at this time in increased amounts. These include corn on the cob, fresh fruits, and bread soaked in either baby food or milk. The last item is perhaps the diet supplement most universally used because problems seem to be few and far between when it is included in the diet. Macaws, however, because of their large size when compared with other psittacines, are more susceptible to calcium deficiencies in their diet. This may lead to their developing brittle bones when fledged. To prevent calcium deficiencies, it is always advisable to have cuttlebone available within the aviary; also Avimin (Lambert Kay) can be added to the food.

Artificial Incubation

If for some reason a pair of macaws prove to be uncertain parents or if the first clutch of eggs is removed to stimulate the pair to lay a second clutch, artificial incubation of the eggs may be attempted. To succeed in incubating parrot eggs by artificial means, those who have limited facilities or experience need to understand a number of factors. It is universally accepted that the first fourteen days of an egg's incubation are the most critical to its development; therefore, whenever possible, eggs should not be removed from the parent birds until at least the fifteenth day of their incubation. Three of the most important factors that affect incubation are given below.

Temperature

Eggs need an extremely constant temperature to hatch successfully. Most people now agree that the ideal temperature for incubating macaw eggs is 99.3°F (37.4°C), although any temperature between 97.9°F and 100.4°F (36.6° and 38°C) will usually achieve success as long as the temperature is kept constant throughout the course of the incubation.

Weight Loss

An egg should lose weight during the incubation process because water is lost from the egg through evaporation and is replaced by a growing air sac normally situated inside at the base of the egg. The oxygen inside the air sac is used during hatching by the developed chick to gain the strength necessary to break through the egg shell. The correct rate of water loss is essential if the chick is to hatch in good health. When the egg loses too much water too quickly, the air sac will grow larger than is normal, which will restrict the space for the developing chick. This in turn can lead to failure in hatching or result in small, weak chicks which usually have severe problems in assimilating calcium and soon die. On the other hand, if the egg does not lose enough water the reverse is true. The air sac may not grow sufficiently to hold enough oxygen for the chick to hatch. Also, the chick will have to absorb the excess albumen before hatching. Humidity is the factor that directly affects the rate at which water evaporates from the egg. Too high a level of humidity surrounding the egg will slow the rate at which water is lost from the egg because the air is already saturated with moisture, whereas a drier atmosphere will lead to a greater rate of water loss. To develop appropriately, the egg should lose between 13 percent to 18 percent of its initial weight, from the time it is laid to the time the chick pips by breaking through into the air sac inside the egg. When an egg is removed from the nest box after the fifteenth day of incubation, the pattern of weight loss is set and little, apart from excessive extremes of incubator humidity, will cause it to deviate from hatching successfully. In the case where an egg is to be artificially incubated from an earlier stage in its development, however, its progress must be carefully monitored and some control of the rate of water loss may be required. The weight of the egg can be measured at regular intervals; its development also can be checked against a weight loss graph or by using the following equation.

$$\frac{\text{Fresh laid egg weight x desired percentage of loss to pip}}{\text{Number of days to pip}}$$

The number of days until pip is normally two days less than the full incubation period. The result of this equation is the daily amount of weight that should be lost by the egg if it is to hatch successfully.

Egg Turning

In brooding her eggs, a hen rotates and moves them randomly. Egg turning is important for several reasons, of which the most important are that it aids water loss, ensures that the yolk does not stick to one particular piece of shell, and allows the developing veins to spread more easily in the albumen. Artificial incubation must therefore simulate the turning actions of the hen. Most manufactured incubators are frequently equipped with turning devices such as the commonly seen tilting tray. This tray has proved highly successful in the hatching of domestic species of birds and poultry, but psittacine eggs with their much smaller yolk and larger albumen content than that of the other species need to be turned more often for the yolk to develop and for the albumen space to be properly used up. It is then best to turn eggs by hand at least seven times a day at two-hour intervals. This is most effectively done by rotating the rounded end of the egg over its pointed axis, always in alternating directions.

As the egg goes through its incubation period its development can be monitored by "candling" the egg. This is done by shining a directed light source into the egg to illuminate the interior. Although growth rates can vary, there are definite signs that become visible at certain stages of the egg's development. By the fifth day of incubation there is clear evidence of the egg's fertility—a small red dot with a sharp red circle surrounding it. Growth can be clearly seen by the tenth day, as well as veins extending widely down one side of the egg. At about the twenty-fourth day the shadow of the chick's bill pushing into the membrane of the air sac should be visible if the chick has not already broken through.

After the chick has broken the air sac it is time to move the egg from the incubator to the hatcher. At this stage the egg needs to be handled in three different ways. First, the egg is no longer turned. Second, once the chick begins to pip and break through the exterior shell the rate of water evapora-

Breeding Macaws

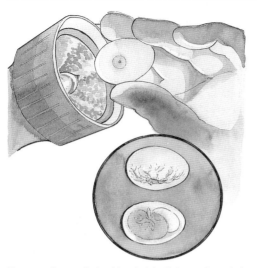

Eggs can be candled with a bright light to show their current stage of development.

tion from the egg will rapidly increase so the hatcher is kept as humid as possible to prevent the chick from drying out while it is struggling to hatch. Third, toward the end of its incubation period, the chick is almost fully formed and begins to generate its own body heat as it starts its hatching struggle. For this reason, hatchers are run at about one degree lower in temperature than the incubator; otherwise, the extra heat generated by the chick's exertions together with the high level of humidity could soon tire the chick which would then find it difficult to complete hatching. After hatching, the chick should be allowed to dry for two to three hours before removing it to a brooder that has been prepared in advance to begin hand rearing.

Hand Rearing Macaws

The preparation for hand rearing a macaw takes place well in advance of the estimated date of its hatching. When newly hatched, although most as-

pects of its biology are fully functional, a macaw is unable to control its body temperature and is extremely weak. The young bird cannot hold itself upright or feed without considerable assistance. Therefore, matters such as appropriate housing, temperature control, diet, feeding schedule, and hygiene must be considered in advance because immediately upon leaving the hatcher the chick will require constant attention from the rearer who should have everything the chick needs ready and waiting.

Housing

Because the newly hatched macaw is unable to properly control either its movement or body temperature, it will need to be housed inside a brooder where both these functions can be controlled for it. There are now many commercially available brooders which will all prove successful if the manufacturer's instructions are followed. Alternatively, a well-ventilated incubator can be converted for this use, provided it has plenty of headroom to accommodate both the young macaw as it grows and the container that will hold the bird. It is also important to check that there are no exposed wires or other potentially dangerous objects that the young macaw might reach and chew. Whatever type of brooder is used, it should be easy to maintain because strict and regular cleaning and disinfecting is required. The brooder must be set up and

A brooder can be used to keep a chick at a constant steady temperature during the early part of its life.

running for several days prior to the hatch date so that the stability of the temperature can be checked. Inside the brooder the macaw must be placed in a small waterproof, easy-to-clean container such as a plastic margarine tub. The bottom of this container needs to be covered with absorbent paper, which should be changed at every feeding and examined to ensure that the chick is passing waste normally. Absorbent paper is also freely used to pad every side of the container to allow the chick to comfortably lean against the side to help it support itself. This propping is particularly important after a chick has been fed because the weight of the food inside its crop can severely unbalance the young chick. Humidity is not an important factor within the brooder; normal room humidity is more than adequate. In the first few days after hatching, however, when the brooder temperature is at its highest level and the newly emerged chick is at its weakest, it may be a safe precaution to place a small shallow dish of water in the brooder to prevent dehydration. All soiled absorbent paper must be replaced and the plastic tub and interior brooder surfaces must be regularly cleaned with a disinfectant wipe.

Temperature

The brooder must be kept at an appropriate temperature for the young macaw to thrive. As a general guide, the initial temperature in the brooder needs to be about 98°F (36.5°C) and should be decreased half a degree daily until the temperature in the brooder nears the room temperature as the chick becomes feathered and strong enough to begin regulating its own body temperature. Every chick is different, however, so the temperature level must be adjusted to suit the individual chick. At the correct temperature, the young bird will have a healthy general light pink color and sleep easily but become highly active and feed strongly at feeding times. In too cold a brooder the chick will have a paler complexion, lose interest in food, become inactive and may even shiver. A chick that is kept too warm will have a reddish body color, become

overactive, regurgitate its food, and look extremely uncomfortable and unsettled.

Diet

Many different rearing diets are used by macaw breeders around the world with apparent success. Obviously then, the "correct" diet is a case of finding one that proves successful and then becoming accustomed to using it. Nevertheless, the following guidelines may be helpful: At the beginning, young chicks require a very liquid diet to enable them to easily digest the food; otherwise, food may become compacted in the crop or stomach. As the chick grows, it can handle food of a more solid consistency. Getting the appropriate density is the one factor that can determine whether a particular diet will prove successful to someone using it for the first time. Following is a diet used by many breeders. It has successfully reared a large number of macaws for several years.

- Three parts pre-soaked monkey chow (25% protein type).
- One part mixed fruit and vegetables (e.g. apple, banana, pear, papaya, and boiled carrots). All fruit should be peeled.

This mixture should be blended with some water until it is of a runny texture. It should then be strained for the first ten days before being fed.

After fourteen days sunflower seed should be husked and ground into the mixture.

This diet should be fed at a temperature of about 100°F (40°C). This formula should be made up fresh for each feed as once blended and warmed it can prove to be a perfect medium for bacterial growth.

Feeding

When first removed from the hatcher to the brooder, a young macaw must not be given its initial feeding for several hours. This is to allow the chick to dry off and regain its strength after hatching; the delay also helps ensure that the majority of the remaining yolk sac has been used before oral

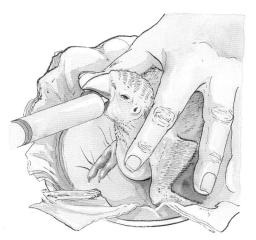

Young macaw chicks should be fed slowly. Be careful not to overfill the crop.

feeding begins. An exception to this rule may be a chick that has been weakened by a prolonged and difficult hatch. Such a chick can be given a small amount of very liquid food a couple of hours earlier; in an emergency even some glucose in warm water can be fed to the young bird soon after it is moved to the brooder. Once begun, subsequent feedings with a very liquid mixture must follow every two hours, from 6:00 A.M. to 12:00 P.M., every day. It is important when feeding that the chick's crop never be overfilled (look out for a stretched and shiny appearance) as this may lead to problems. At each feeding, it is essential to check that the crop is completely empty of food; if there is food still present, no further food should be given until this has gone. Food that will not leave the crop after a reasonable length of time is a possible sign of an impacted crop; to alleviate this condition some warm, slightly saline water must be given. If this remedy does not help, the chick will require the immediate assistance of a veterinarian to survive. It is always safer to be cautious and feed the chick a mixture that is more liquid than solid. Later, as the young bird grows and becomes stronger, its food can gradually be made thicker. This will mean that the time between feedings can be lengthened accordingly as the chick will take longer to digest the thicker mixture. It should be standard practice throughout the course of rearing to thoroughly clean the chick after each feeding because excess food that is left around the bird's face can lead to skin irritation and possible disease.

Weaning

Hand-reared macaws may be weaned to a regular diet between the ages of ten weeks to eight months, depending on the individual bird. The diet should become more liquid and the birds should be offered slices of soft fruit, soaked seeds and millet sprays, which they can pick at. Weaning can be a long and difficult process and success is usually dependent upon the breeder's patience. Spend time playing with your birds and teaching them about new foods. A lonely, bored macaw is much harder to wean than an active, inquisitive one. Weaning must proceed at the individual bird's pace. It should never be rushed. If problems should occur, do not hesitate to seek help at an early stage.

Chicks should be weighed daily and a record of their growth should be kept.

Breeding Macaws

Growth

Macaws generally take about 16 weeks to fledge but when hand reared they may take longer. Weaning is also usually prolonged in hand-reared birds as they do not readily help themselves to food even when they are hungry. A chick's progress can be measured by weighing it and then comparing its growth to the growth curve in the accompanying illustration. As the chick grows, it will gain weight steadily throughout the day as it is fed, then lose some of this gain as it sleeps at night. For this reason, the chick should always be weighed at the same time each day, preferably before the first morning feeding. After three to four weeks of age, the young bird will need to have more freedom of movement to allow it to exercise and strengthen its legs. At this time, small twigs or some other type of floor covering can be added to the bottom of the container to give the chick's feet something to grip, thereby encouraging correct development of the feet.

Weight Gain of a Green-winged Macaw

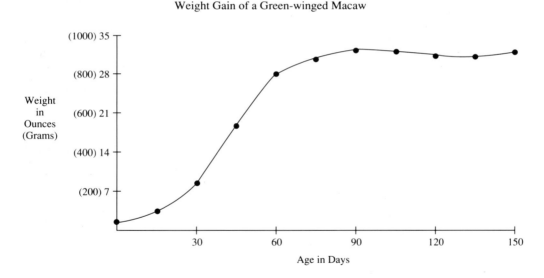

This graph showing the weight gain of a green-winged macaw can be used as a rough guide to the shape of weight-gain curve that can be expected of any macaw chicks during the hand-rearing period.

Macaw Species

Genus *Ara*

The genus *Ara* contains 13 living species of macaw, with at least two known species believed to be extinct—the St. Croix macaw (*Ara autocthones*) and the Cuban macaw (*Ara tricolor*). At the time of writing this book, the blue-headed or Coulon's macaw (*Ara couloni*) is known to still exist in the wild; however, it is seriously threatened, leaving its future greatly in doubt.

The 13 species vary greatly in size and color, although all share a similar shape: Aras have long, graduated tail feathers and large broad heads with bills that are ample and pronounced. The most noticeable taxonomic feature of birds of this genus is the area of bare skin on both sides of the face. The facial patches can be either completely bare or to some degree covered by rows of small facial feathers, depending on which species is being viewed. All species are monomorphic, meaning there are no distinct visual differences between the sexes (male and female look exactly alike).

Green-winged Macaw
Ara chloroptera
CITES Appendix II

Description: With an overall length of 36 inches (90 cm), this is the largest species in the genus. Color of plumage covering the head, throat, breast, stomach, thighs, upper back, and lesser wing coverts is a rich, dark red. Green covers much of the central band of the wing, including the inner secondaries, tertials, and scapulars, giving the bird its common name. The remainder of the wing feathers—the primaries, secondaries, and greater wing coverts—are a dark blue with a lighter blue also covering the lower back, rump, upper- and undertail coverts and the tips of the red tail feathers. The facial area is bare with the exception of several rows of very small feathers, giving the impression of thin red lines painted on the bare pale skin. The upper mandible is light gray with darker edging at the lower bases; the lower mandible is black. Legs are gray. The iris is pale yellow.

Distribution: It has a wide range across much of northern South America, including eastern Panama, northwestern Colombia east of the Andes, Venezuela, the Guianas, northern Brazil, northern and eastern Bolivia, and eastern Paraguay.

Habitat and Status: It can be encountered in a variety of habitats across its range, but is perhaps most at home in primary humid lowland forests up to 3,300 feet (1,000 m) above sea level. This species, although extremely widespread, is noted for being less gregarious than other species; therefore it is rarely seen in large flocks. Yet, it is possibly the most widely distributed and numerous of the wild macaws. Because of its less sociable nature this species may well need a much larger area of land to sustain a viable population over a long period of time when compared to some of the more communal species. For this reason, improper land management could adversely threaten the future of this bird within a surprisingly short time, despite the apparent large populations and wide range it still covers in the wild.

Aviculture: The green-winged macaw is well established in captivity. With breeding now being successfully achieved regularly in collections around the world, its future must surely be secure in captivity. It is known to have appeared in aviculture as far back as the seventeenth century, although, as with most species of captive parrots, large-scale captive breeding did not occur regularly until the late 1970s and early 1980s. It is not the most widely kept and bred of the available species and is perhaps often passed over in favor of some of the slightly more colorful species. This oversight is a shame as most people who work with this species find that it has a somewhat quieter and more affectionate nature than others. The slightly larger size also gives this bird a much more impressive appearance, particularly in relation to the head and bill, which are extremely pronounced and imposing. Hand-reared green-winged macaws, if obtained young and given the attention and affection they require, will prove one of the best house pet birds among the macaws, provided proper thought has been given in advance to their size and potentially destructive bills.

Breeding: When compared to other species, wild-caught green-winged macaws take longer (several years) to settle in captivity and require more time to select a mate and form a strong pair bond. Captive-bred green-winged macaws, however, pair with their mates with seemingly greater confidence than their wild counterparts, and they show signs of breeding much quicker; in addition, they generally prove to be more prolific as breeding pairs. Two or three eggs is the normal clutch size; incubation takes approximately 28 days and the hen begins to sit as soon as the first egg has been laid. After hatching, if left with the parents, the chick will start to fledge at around 14 weeks of age; however, in the case of hand-reared birds weaning and independence may take considerably longer to achieve.

Scarlet Macaw
Ara macao
CITES Appendix I

Description: Overall length is 33 inches (85 cm). Its general appearance is similar to that of the green-winged macaw but it is smaller and can easily be distinguished by the broad yellow band running across the wing over the greater and medium wing coverts. Main body plumage is a noticeably lighter shade of red than that of the green-winged macaw. This red extends over most of the body, with the exceptions of the lower back, rump, and upper- and undertail coverts, which are light blue. A darker blue covers most of the flight feathers as well as the tips of the yellow wing coverts and the red tail feathers. Its face is bare with a few small feathers showing on the pale skin. The bill is creamy gray on the upper mandible but darkens to black at the base; its lower mandible is black. The legs are gray and the iris, brown.

Distribution: There are two recognized populations of scarlet macaws: the yellow-winged, Central American population—from the state of Oaxaca in Mexico southward to southern Panama—and the South American population—ranging east of the Andes, from Colombia to Bolivia, and eastward across Brazil to Guiana and the island of Trinidad.

Habitat and Status: Like the green-winged macaw, this species is most frequently encountered below 3,300 feet (1,000 m) above sea level, either in humid dense forests or in more open secondary forests and woodlands. Although widely distributed, the scarlet macaw is becoming increasingly rare across much of its range, particularly Central America. This species as much as others has been adversely affected by the trapping activities for the pet market. Although its range may appear to be extensive, much of this area is in fact now devoid of resident populations of these birds, which are usually found grouped in colonies in the more secure and less disturbed areas of the countries mentioned.

Aviculture: The scarlet macaw for the last hundred years has been perhaps the best known of all South American parrots in captivity and is frequently described by aviculturists as the most beautiful and striking. Despite early problems in the captive breeding of this species associated with the incorrect sexing and difficult adaptability of wild-caught birds, its future in captivity now appears secure. Since the late 1970s with the advent of more reliable sexing techniques this species is now widely bred. Young hand-reared birds can make good pets but require much of their owners' time and attention because they can often become more boisterous and aggressive as they mature. Such birds lose their tameness and are never completely trustworthy and are therefore best paired up for breeding.

Breeding: With captive-bred birds now readily available for pairing success the breeding of scarlet macaws has widely spread. The most important factor in the success of a pair would appear to be the strength of the bond the birds develop; therefore, the birds should be given as much choice as possible when selecting a mate. Often, although many captive birds are available, there may be a larger number of one or the other sex. In the case of this species, there is often a surplus of males in the market. Therefore, it is best to buy a bird that has already been sexed to avoid spending the next several years trying to breed two birds of the same sex. The clutch usually consists of two to four eggs; the incubation time is about 26 days for each egg. Parent-reared young start to fledge in 75 to 82 days, whereas hand-reared young may take up to 110 or 120 days because of the prolonged weaning period in all hand-reared macaws.

Blue and Gold Macaw
(Also called Blue and Yellow Macaw)
Ara ararauna
CITES Appendix II

Description: Overall length is 34 inches (86 cm). Most of the upper body, from the crown of the head reaching right down the back and over the upperwings and tail, is blue. The undertail coverts are also blue. The front of the crown is greenish blue and the forehead green. The undersides of the body are nearly all a rich yellow; this color covers the entire breast, stomach, thighs, and reaches up the sides of the face to the bare skin around the eye. The only other main coloration is a black patch that reaches around the underside of the bird's throat. The bare skin on the side of the face has several fine lines of small black feathers; the bill is also completely black. The legs are dark gray and the iris, yellow.

Distribution: It is widely distributed over northern South America in Colombia, southern Venezuela, Brazil, the Guianas, Trinidad, northern Bolivia, northern Peru, eastern Panama, and Ecuador.

Habitat and Status: Definitely a bird of lowland forests, the blue and gold macaw is rarely found above 1,650 feet (500 m) in altitude; it prefers humid primary forest areas, although occasionally it will choose secondary forests, depending on food availability. This is perhaps the most numerous and secure of all the wild macaw populations. Captive breeding has considerably reduced the trade in wild-caught birds, although some are still imported because they command a lower price than that of captive-bred birds. This species, along with the green-winged macaw, is the least regulated of the large macaws; therefore, stricter controls are needed to further diminish the selling of wild-caught birds.

Aviculture: The blue and gold is by far the most widely seen, kept, and bred of all the macaws kept in captivity. It has been known in aviculture since the eighteenth century with the first breeding being recorded as long ago as 1818. Although problems were frequently encountered in early aviculture with sexing this species, once established pairs began to breed they proved extremely prolific. Therefore, they have been bred with relative frequency even during the 100 years prior to the introduction of more reliable sexing techniques, artificial incubation, and the better rearing routines established over the last 20 years. Young hand-reared birds can make good pets, although to remain tame they require much attention if their rather individual and boisterous temperaments are to be moderated.

Breeding: As already stated, this species has been and is bred with frequency in collections throughout the world. Of particular interest is a certain adaptability this bird has shown when incubating its eggs: In hot countries such as Spain, parent birds incubate their eggs up to three days less than is the case for birds in cooler climates as, for example, that of Scandinavia. The most common incubation time, particularly when the eggs are incubated artificially, is 26 days. The size of the clutch is between two to four eggs. This species is noted for the willingness displayed by established pairs to produce three and sometimes four clutches in the same year if eggs are pulled. It is important, however, that all macaws be given the chance to rear young at least once a year. Young chicks reared by their parents fledge at 14 weeks of age, but hand-reared chicks take much longer to become independent.

Blue-throated Macaw
(Also called Caninde Macaw)
Ara glaucogularis
(formerly, *Ara caninde*)
CITES Appendix I

Description: Overall size is 33 inches (85 cm). It is at first sight similar to the blue and gold macaw, but it can easily be distinguished by the throat markings: the throat patch is blue, as its common name implies, and is considerably larger than the black patch of the blue and gold. Most of the upper body, including the wings and tail, are a light blue which in sunlight acquires a greenish tinge. Other than the throat, the underside of the body is light orange, as are the undertail coverts. The bare facial area has several rows of fine blue feathers. The bill and legs are a dull grayish black. The iris is yellow.

Distribution: The blue-throated has quite a restricted range and comes mainly from the eastern area of Bolivia (Beni and Santa Cruz Department).

Habitat and Status: Within its region, this bird is mainly confined to humid and dense lowland forest areas or more open secondary forests, usually close to water. In the wild, the bird is extremely threatened: Over the past hundred years, its wild population was restricted by its limited range to about 1,000 birds. This number has been seriously reduced by trapping, particularly in the early 1980s when the species first appeared in aviculture. Although trapping has decreased since then, the wild population presently has less than 400 individuals.

Aviculture: This species was practically unknown until the late 1970s, and the first breeding only occurred as recently as 1984. This bird is far from being established in captivity. Much effort will be required to breed enough of these birds from different blood lines to obtain a viable, self-sustaining captive population. For this reason, the blue-throated is unlikely to be considered as a pet bird in the near future, if ever. As an avicultural bird, it is extremely beautiful and appears much more elegant; moreover, it moves less clumsily than other large macaws. It is therefore understandable why so many aviculturists would wish to keep and breed this species. One can hope that in the future enough captive-bred birds will be produced to allow more people to keep them.

Breeding: Although this species has now been bred in as many as ten collections in different parts of the world, breeding cannot yet be described as regular and is by no means widespread. The clutch of two to four eggs reportedly takes about 26 days to incubate and breeding does not appear to differ too greatly from that of other macaws as, for example, the blue and gold. Breeding, however, presently appears to be limited by two factors: First, the rarity and high value of the species restricts the number of birds kept by an aviculturist, thereby reducing the opportunities for natural mate selection and social interaction for the macaws outside the breeding season. Second, the majority of pairs are still of wild-caught origin and may be proving more cautious and reserved when compared to captive-bred birds of other species. Perhaps after enough blue-throated macaws have been bred in captivity and they themselves start to breed, their regularity and prolificity in breeding will dramatically increase.

Military Macaw
Ara militaris
CITES Appendix I

Description: Overall length is 27 to 29 inches (70–75 cm). Most of the body is predominantly green; this color merges with blue toward the lower back, rump, and undertail coverts. The flight feathers, too, are a greenish blue; the underside of the tail feathers is an olive green, and the upper side, a brownish red. The other noticeable coloration is the bright red band across the bird's forehead. The facial skin is bare apart from faint lines of black feathers running across it. The bill is a dull gray, as are the legs. The iris is yellow.

Three subspecies have been recognized, although none are visually distinct from one another.

Distribution: The three main macaw populations that are regarded as subspecies are geographically separated from each other. *A. m. militaris* occurs from northwestern Venezuela to eastern Ecuador and northern Peru; *A. m. mexicana* is found throughout Mexico, except in the rain forest zones; and *A. m. boliviana* inhabits the tropical zones of Bolivia and the northernmost region of Argentina.

Habitat and Status: The military macaw is known to occupy more open and exposed areas than the other species so far mentioned. In Mexico it can be found in semiarid, open countryside, although rarely too far away from water. It can also be seen at much higher altitudes of up to 8,000 feet (2,500 m). The wild populations of all three subspecies appear stable, although their future depends on appropriate land management of those regions. Limitations imposed on the trade of wild-caught military macaws have been effective and nearly all available macaws are captive bred.

Aviculture: The military macaw is well established in captivity, particularly in the United States, although it has never shared the popularity of the brighter colored species. It is therefore less commonly exhibited with fewer breeders concentrating on it, making the military macaw's price slightly higher than that of the more popular large macaws. Despite this, enough macaws are bred to supply the demand for them; moreover, this bird has kept pace with the increased general interest in parrots. Because of its unexciting coloration, only a limited number of militaries have been bred for the pet market. Nevertheless, I find that even hand-reared birds are generally moody and not completely trustworthy as pets. This species is best when kept mainly for breeding.

Breeding: Although well established in aviculture, the military appears to have had much less effort put into its captive breeding than other more brightly colored macaws. The first captive breedings were not recorded until the 1960s. Most of the birds being presently produced are intended for breeding. Therefore, to accommodate breeders' preferences, the young birds are left to be reared by the parent birds, as opposed to their being reared by hand when intended for the pet market. Moreover, hand rearing of young macaws is usually carried out in an effort to maximize egg production, not to produce tame birds. The clutch size of militaries is two or three eggs, although a fourth egg is possible. Incubation takes 26 days, and the young fledge after about 90 days of parent rearing.

Buffon's Macaw
(Also called Great Green Macaw)
Ara ambigua
CITES Appendix I

Description: Overall length is 33 inches (85 cm). Although visually similar to the military macaw, the Buffon's is noticeably larger; also, its overall body coloring is of a much lighter yellowish green. Most of the body is light green and turns blue around the lower back, rump, and undertail coverts. The forehead carries a broad scarlet band and the tail is red tipped, with blue above and olive yellow below. The facial skin is bare except for several fine lines of small black feathers. The bill is grayish black and becomes paler toward the tip. The legs are dark gray. The iris is yellow.

Two subspecies of the Buffon's macaw are recognized which are distinguishable from each other only by slight size and color differences.

Distribution: The Buffon's macaw has two main populations, one running through Central America from southeastern Honduras down to western Colombia, which is the nominate race

(*A. a. ambigua*), and the other occupying western Ecuador, which is disputed to be a separate subspecies (*A. a. guayaquilensis*).

Aviculture: The Buffon's macaw is not widely established in captivity, unlike the similar military macaw. It is considered a rarity and as such commands a high price, despite good breeding results being achieved by aviculturists fortunate enough to house them. If the present levels of effort and breeding are maintained, it looks as if the Buffon's macaw will indeed be established firmly in captivity, its present limited numbers not withstanding. I have worked with only a small number of captive-bred birds of this species but have found them to be extremely well natured and gentle, even when paired in breeding aviaries. Despite their seemingly good temperament and although I suspect they would be among the best adapted, the Buffon's macaw is far too rare to allow birds to be kept as pets. In the near future, at least all available birds will be needed to ensure that this species does indeed become firmly established in captivity.

Breeding: This species is not widely kept and bred; nevertheless, people working with this species, in particular with first-generation captive birds, are obtaining encouraging breeding results. Their successes suggest that the Buffon's macaw, once established in strong pair bonds, can be extremely prolific and, if settled, can breed regularly. The clutch consists of two to four eggs. The incubation period is about 26 days. Young Buffon's usually leave the nest in as little as 84 days.

Red-fronted Macaw (Also called Red-cheeked or Lafresnaye's Macaw)
Ara rubrogenys
CITES Appendix I

Description: Overall length is 24 inches (60 cm). The main overall body color is olive green, which becomes brighter toward the head and shoulders. The forehead, crown, spot behind the eye, and thighs are all red; the bend of wing, lesser wing coverts, and underwing coverts are orange to red.

The tail is olive green and tipped with blue above and olive yellow below. The facial area of bare skin is smaller than that of some of the other species and is pinkish white. The bill is grayish black, as are the legs. The iris is orange.

Distribution: This species has a very limited range that is confined inside the perimeters of southern-central Bolivia, between the cities of Santa Cruz and Cochabamba.

Aviculture: The red-fronted macaw was unknown in aviculture until the mid-1970s or later, and enough birds only became readily available in the early 1980s. They are still rare and cannot be said to be widely established; nevertheless, the early breeding pairs of red-fronted macaws proved highly productive. Although the number of people keeping them is still small, these macaws are presently being bred quite regularly. One breeder in the United Kingdom is producing over 20 macaws a year from his four to five adult pairs and has produced a total of 100 birds. Their value is now about the same level as that of the other large macaws. They are likely to become more widely established because their small size makes them attractive to the aviculturists who do not have room for the larger macaws. This species is also regarded as one of the hardiest of the macaws, coming as it does from colder and more exposed mountain regions. Although some hand-reared birds are being sold as pets and seem to settle well, the rarity of this macaw and the extreme threat to it in the wild means that this species, at least for the near future, should only be kept for breeding.

Breeding: Although only fairly recently arrived in aviculture and only bred in captivity for the first time in 1978, the red-fronted macaw is being bred well. Their small size makes them easier to accommodate than the preceding species. Two or three eggs are generally laid; these take 26 days to incubate. Red-fronted chicks fledge after 84 days, although because of their rarity most young birds are hand reared and take longer to wean and become independent.

Macaw Species

Severe Macaw (Also called Chestnut-fronted Macaw)

Ara severa
CITES Appendix II

Description: Overall length is 19 inches (49 cm). The main body color is green, which becomes bluish over the top of the head. Bordering the bare facial area a bit of brown runs down the sides of the cheeks and under the chin and also forms a band across the forehead. Chestnut brown can also be found on the tips of the breast feathers, giving this bird its alternate common name. There is red on the outer primaries, bend of wing, and carpal edge; red can also be found on the underwing coverts, although most of the underwing is olive brown. The primary coverts on the upperwing are blue. The tail is reddish brown above but becomes green toward the base and blue toward the tip; the underside of the tail is reddish orange. The bare skin on the face is white and has fine black lines running across it. The bill is dark gray, as are the legs. The iris is yellow. A subspecies has in the past been described, but it is not distinguishable from the nominate species other than by a slightly larger size. It is not widely recognized.

Distribution: The severe macaw can be found from eastern Panama to the Guianas and from northeastern Brazil south to Bolivia, frequenting palm groves near rivers.

Habitat and Status: Known to prefer open forests, the severe macaw inhabits primary and secondary forest areas, forest edges, and open woodlands across its wide natural range. It is nearly always found below altitudes of 5,000 feet (1,500 m). Because of its large range and the fact that it has not until recently been as adversely affected by trapping for the pet trade as the large macaws, its status and future conservation outlook seem fairly secure; nevertheless, continued deforestation will pose the greatest future threat.

Aviculture: The severe macaw has never been a common bird in aviculture outside of the United States into which it was imported in fairly large numbers in the 1980s. Elsewhere in the world, in recent years small imports were made and breeding has occurred. People who have worked with this species have found it soon became a favorite in a collection, so the severe has received concentrated attention from several breeders and has benefited from this, despite the still limited number of birds that are available in most countries. Hand-reared severe macaws prove to be delightful pets, although they are not likely to be readily available and usually command high prices.

Breeding: The small number of adults of this species that are available has restricted the chances of the severe macaw to become more widely bred and established. The clutch consists of two or three eggs which take 25 days to incubate. Eggs can be laid at two- or three-day intervals. The young spend up to 12 weeks in the nest box before fledging. Hand-rearing has also been achieved successfully, but with young taking up to five months before they are completely weaned and independent.

Yellow-collared Macaw (Also called Yellow-naped Macaw)

Ara auricollis
CITES Appendix II

Description: Overall length is 15 inches (38 cm). The main body color is green. The forehead, crown, and lower cheeks are brown. This bird gets its common name from the yellow collar that extends around the hindneck. There is also some blue on the upperwings, mainly on the primaries. The tail is blue at the tip and becomes reddish brown toward the base; the underside of the tail is yellow, as is the underside of the flight feathers. The bare facial area is creamy white and the bill is a dark gray that turns lighter toward the tip. The legs are pink and the iris is orange.

Distribution: The yellow-collared macaw can be found in an area stretching from the northern and eastern regions of Bolivia, east into Brazil, and south into northern Paraguay to northwestern Argentina. More isolated populations also inhabit the central areas of Brazil.

Habitat and Status: This species is reported to inhabit widely differing habitats such as humid forests, woodlands, and even agricultural lands. It is still quite common and abundant in most areas across its natural range and adapts well to human disturbance; therefore, it could possibly be one of the most securely established species in the wild, where it can still be seen in large flocks.

Aviculture: This macaw had always been rare in aviculture prior to its large-scale importation during the 1970s; after this, it became fairly easily available at moderate prices. Presently, however, prices have increased because of recent curtailments on the importation of this species. The yellow-collared macaw is liberally bred by the people who keep them, but it is well established only in the United States. Its numbers are increasing through aviculture; this is good news not only because it is an interesting and unique aviary bird but also because it is among the macaws best suited for the pet market. When hand-reared, this macaw can become extremely tame; despite its smaller size, however, when compared with other macaws its voice is still strong and harsh.

Breeding: Since its appearance in aviculture, the yellow-collared macaw has been successfully bred by many. After the first breeding, most pairs go on to become regular and prolific breeders. This species has shown it will accept nest boxes in a variety of sizes and shapes, but the basic factors of security, light requirements, and size of entrance hole still apply. The usual clutch size is three to four eggs, which are laid at two- or three-day intervals and take 25 days to incubate. The young normally fledge after the tenth week inside the nest box.

Red-bellied Macaw
Ara manilata
CITES Appendix II

Description: Overall length is 20 inches (50 cm). The overall body plumage is green but is tinged with olive over the neck, back, rump, uppertail coverts, and lower underparts. The crown and the lower cheeks have a bluish tinge, as do the primaries and primary coverts in the wing and the undersides of the tail feathers. The throat and breast feathers are gray but edged with green. A broad red patch covers the lower abdomen down to the vent and gives this bird its common name and most distinctive visual feature; the feathers of the thighs are also edged with red. The bare facial area is yellow and the bill is grayish black, as are the legs. The iris is dark brown.

Distribution: This species spreads widely throughout northern South America, from the Guianas through northern and southeastern Venezuela to Colombia, then south to eastern Peru, northern Bolivia, and Brazil. It can also be found on the island of Trinidad.

Habitat and Status: This is a bird of lowland, humid forests and is rarely found in more open exposed habitats. For this reason and despite its extensive natural range, it is mainly confined to areas of undisturbed forest; therefore, it is not as widespread and secure as its range would suggest. Additionally, field work revealed that it may well be extremely dependent on the fruit of one species of palm when rearing its young. This contingency could in the future severely threaten this species if the primary forests within its range are disturbed by humans.

Aviculture: The red-bellied macaw is presently in the curious position of being the most inexpensive and the easiest to obtain of the macaw species and at the same time still not being well established

Top: A hyacinthine macaw *(Anodorhynchus hyacinthinus)* ▶ waiting for its food.
Bottom: Large macaws like this hyacinthine should be handled with extreme care. The head is controlled by a hand around the back of the head, with the thumb and first finger securing each side of the lower mandible.

Macaw Species

in captivity. Wild-caught red-bellies prove nervous and difficult to breed in captivity. Among them, deaths linked to stress often occur; they can either refuse most of the food offered or become addicted to one particular food, such as sunflower seed, and refuse everything else. These problems coupled with the bird's relatively cheap price have caused it to be neglected by the majority of serious breeders; nearly all the birds being offered for sale are therefore wild caught. This species is very much in need of a concentrated effort to produce enough captive-bred birds to establish a firm base to secure a long-term captive population. Perhaps later generations of captive-bred birds will show few of the stress-related problems that are so common in their wild-caught counterparts. Moreover, on the few occasions that I have seen hand-reared young of this species offered for sale, they were extremely tame, leading me to suspect that they would make ideal and affectionate pets. This is definitely not the case with wild-caught specimens.

Breeding: Pairs of wild-caught birds are offered for sale as surgically sexed and at relatively inexpensive prices, yet the red-bellied macaw is not widely bred. Moreover, the first recorded captive breeding was not until 1982! Breeding, at the moment, shows no signs of becoming more widespread, but with the future importation regulations of this species being reviewed the red-bellied macaw, as already pointed out, is in need of a serious breeding effort. Clutch size is two to four eggs; incubation takes 25 days. Young chicks fledge at about 11 weeks of age.

Illiger's Macaw
Ara maracana
CITES Appendix I

Description: Overall length is 17 inches (43 cm). Main body color is green and turns to blue over the top of the head and cheeks. There is a bright red band across the forehead and another across the lower abdomen; the lower back is also red. These red patches make this species quite distinctive. The green of the rump area and uppertail coverts is tinged with olive. The primaries and their coverts are blue, with some blue also on the secondaries. The tail is blue above, becoming reddish toward the base; below, it is olive yellow. The bare facial area is pale yellow and the bill is black. The legs are yellow and the iris, orange.

Distribution: Found widely within Brazil and south through Paraguay to northeastern Argentina.

Habitat and Status: Little study has been done on this species in the wild, but it is thought to mainly inhabit humid, primary forests. Since 1989 it has been listed as CITES I and is among the most strictly protected of all the macaws: no birds can be imported now. The Illiger's macaw is now suspected to be extremely rare across most of its range, with eastern Brazil providing its best stronghold. Moreover, the deforestation within Brazil and across other regions of its range now severely threaten the future of this macaw in its wild state.

Aviculture: This species is well established in captivity. Wild-caught birds that entered aviculture throughout the 1970s and 1980s settled well and have proved to be free breeders; captive-bred birds are therefore available in most countries. Hand-reared young make good pets, but they are highly individual and require much of their owner's time and attention to remain tame and not become boisterous.

Breeding: Up to four eggs are laid in a clutch; incubation takes 24 days. The period between laying each of the eggs is nearly always three days as opposed to the more common two days of the large

Lear's macaw *(Anodorhynchus leari).*

species. This often leads to a ten-day difference in the ages of the chicks in the nest box. In the case of broods with four young that are being parent reared, a close watch should be kept to ensure that the youngest chicks are receiving enough food, particularly in the first week of their lives because they are competing with their much larger older brothers and sisters. The young can start to fledge at around 10 weeks of age.

Blue-headed Macaw
(Also called Coulon's Macaw)
Ara couloni
CITES Appendix I

Description: Overall length is 16 inches (41 cm). Main body plumage is green but becomes slightly more yellowish on the underside of the body. All of the head, with the exception of the bare facial patches is blue, giving the bird its common name and making it highly distinctive. There is also some blue in the wings, mainly on the primaries and their coverts. The tail is blue above and yellow below. The bare facial area is gray; the bill is dark gray, becoming lighter toward the tip. The legs are light brown and the iris is yellow.

Distribution: Formerly, eastern Peru, southwestern Brazil, and northernmost Bolivia. Today's range is uncertain.

Habitat and Status: This macaw is reported to prefer forest edges and open woodland. The size and security of its wild population is unsure and much debated. This species has always been restricted in its range and has never been highly numerous. It has managed nearly completely to avoid being captured for the pet trade; many therefore feel that this small wild population will continue and may even grow larger as long as this is the case. There are other reports, however, that suggest this wild population is rapidly declining and may be, along with the Spix's macaw, the most endangered of all macaws, with the exception of the possibly extinct glaucous macaw.

Aviculture: This species is unknown in modern aviculture. There are only two reports of this macaw being kept in captivity in the early part of this century, one in Germany and the other in the United States.

Breeding: There are no reports of there ever being two blue-headed macaws kept together in captivity. Little is known about their breeding in the wild. It is unlikely that this species will ever be established in captivity.

Hahn's Macaw/Noble Macaw
(Also called Red-shouldered Macaw)
Ara nobilis or *Diopsittaca nobilis*
CITES Appendix II

The nominate race, Hahn's macaw (*A. n. nobilis* or *D. n. nobilis*) is distinct from the second race, noble macaw (*A. n. cumanensis* or *D. n. cumanensis*) by being smaller and having a black bill, as opposed to the pale cream color of the upper mandible of the second race.

Description: Overall lengths are *A. n. nobilis*, 12 inches (30 cm) and *A. n. cumanensis*, 13 inches (34 cm). Main body plumage is green and becomes yellowish in the underpart of the body. The forehead and forecrown are blue, as are the outer primaries on the upperwing. The bend of wing and the underwing coverts are red, giving the bird its alternate common name. The undersides of the flight feathers and tail are olive yellow. The facial area is white. The bill can be completely black in the nominate race, whereas in the subspecies the upper mandible is whitish. Legs are gray. The iris is dark orange.

Distribution: It ranges from the Guianas, eastern Venezuela and southward to southern Brazil, southeastern Peru, and northern Bolivia.

Habitat and Status: This species is known to be common across most of its range and to occupy a wide variety of habitats, but is mostly found in open woodland and forest edges. This species appears to be fairly secure within its wild range, although it could still be affected by large-scale changes in land management within its range.

Macaw Species

Aviculture: This species is well established in captivity, although the subspecies, *A. n. cumanensis*, has been imported from Guyana with a quota of 1,000 birds a year. It has been widely bred, and captive birds are usually freely available. Hand-reared birds make excellent pets and become extremely tame. The two races are quite distinct from each other, so every effort should be made not to interbreed them, especially because the second race is far less established than the nominate one. This bird may well be considered the easiest of all the macaws to care for in captivity and therefore is the ideal species for an inexperienced person to start with.

Breeding: The species has been widely bred for many years in most countries where aviculture is practiced. The clutch can be from two up to five eggs, which take 24 days to incubate. Eggs are laid at two-day intervals, as is the case with the large Ara species. Young chicks can fledge as early as the eighth week. These birds often are willing to double clutch even without the incentive of having its first eggs removed for artificial incubation and chick hand rearing.

Genus *Anodorhynchus*

The genus *Anodorhynchus* contains three species, although one of these, the glaucous macaw, may now be extinct. All three species share the typical macaw shape but are among the largest of the parrots. The facial area is feathered, unlike the Ara species, although there is some bare skin bordering the lower mandible. Additionally, there is a prominent periophthalmic ring.

Hyacinthine Macaw
(Also called Hyacinth Macaw)
Anodorhynchus hyacinthinus
CITES Appendix I

Description: Overall length is 39 inches (100 cm). The entire body is almost completely covered with rich violet plumage. The only contrasting color is the yellow of the rings of bare skin encircling the eye and bordering the lower mandible. The bill is dark gray, as are the legs. The iris is dark brown.

Distribution: The main population is found across northern Brazil, although it has also been recorded in the extreme eastern part of Bolivia and in northern Paraguay.

Habitat and Status: The hyacinthine's preferred habitats are secondary forest and open woodland. This feature makes this species fairly easy to find and observe in the parts of its range where it is numerous. This macaw has probably suffered a more direct slump in its wild population from trapping than any other species. The wild populations of this bird presently must number well below the 3,000 stated in the last survey that was carried out in 1987. Moves to protect it also initiated at that time only created a much increased demand on trapping of the wild population; the excessive trapping is only now being brought under control.

Aviculture: There can be no doubt that the hyacinthine macaw is to many aviculturists the most beautiful and majestic of all parrots. Its intimidating size and powerful bill combine with a gentle but shy nature that make this macaw a favorite of almost every parrot enthusiast. It is uncommon in captivity, although there is a large number of wild-caught, mature birds to form a population base. These wild-caught birds remain nervous for many years, however, and need seclusion and gentle care if they are to breed. Captive-bred birds by comparison, although not yet widely available, are normally inquisitive and outgoing; moreover, some young captive-bred pairs have proved to be free breeding and confident. The hyacinthine's pet potential is undoubtedly great; hand-reared birds of this species are not only among the most impressive of all parrots, but also among the most gentle in nature. At present, however, it would be wrong to withhold any mature hyacinthine macaws from the chance of breeding. From 5 years of age onward, every one of these birds should be given every opportunity to pair and breed whenever possible.

Breeding: The hyacinthine macaw is being bred annually in collections around the world, although it is by no means firmly established. Most of the birds now in captivity were imported from the wild during the late 1970s and the 1980s. This species cannot be regarded as being secure in captivity until a larger number of productive, captive-bred pairs exists. Two eggs are generally laid, and occasionally a third one; these take 26 to 28 days to incubate. Because of the rarity of captive-bred young, most hyacinthine chicks are usually hand reared, which is an extremely long process with this species as weaning often takes approximately 150 days to complete.

Glaucous Macaw
Anodorynchus glaucus
CITES Appendix I

Description: Overall length is 28 inches (72 cm). The glaucous macaw resembles the larger hyacinthine macaw, except that its overall body coloration, particularly the wings and tail, is lighter and of a greenish-blue.

Distribution: Known only from a restricted area in southeastern Brazil, northwestern Uruguay, and northern Paraguay but has not been officially sighted in the wild for over a hundred years.

Habitat and Status: No information is available regarding the natural history of the glaucous macaw, but, if it still lives, it is within the large undisturbed areas of primary forest in the southern part of Brazil. This species has not been officially sighted for a long time, but this does not automatically mean that it is extinct. It is entirely possible that isolated populations within the interior of northern Brazil still exist as has been rumored fairly recently.

Aviculture: Only a handful of glaucous macaws have ever been held in captivity. The last one, reported in 1938, was in an Argentina zoo. Other macaws have since been rumored to be captive but none have been verified.

Breeding: This species has never been bred in captivity and no observations have been made of its breeding habits in the wild.

Lear's Macaw
Anodorhynchus leari
CITES Appendix I

Description: Overall length is 30 inches (75 cm). The Lear's macaw, but for its smaller size, closely resembles the hyacinthine macaw. It has the same deep blue coloration, unlike the lighter color of the glaucous macaw. Apart from its size, another difference is the larger area of bare yellow skin bordering the lower mandible.

Distribution: Known only in a restricted area within northeastern Brazil.

Habitat and Status: This species inhabits only a restricted area of forest within its range. The wild population is thought to number about a hundred birds or fewer. It is one of the most endangered of the macaws.

Aviculture: There are less than 20 captive Lear's macaws. Four of those individuals are in the United States, many others are in Brazil. At the time of writing no breeding pairs of this species exist in captivity; its future in aviculture is therefore extremely doubtful.

Breeding: The only known captive breeding of this species is one by a pair in Busch Gardens in Tampa that first bred in 1982 and again several times later with limited success. The female of that breeding pair has since died. The future of this species in captivity and perhaps also in the wild depends heavily upon bringing the few remaining captive birds together.

Genus *Cyanopsitta*

Cyanopsitta is a monotypic genus containing a single species, *Cyanopsitta spixii*, the Spix's macaw. Physically it resembles all macaws, but is of medium size and has a graduated tail; it can easily be distinguished by its light blue plumage and feathered cheek patches. This species is distinct from all other macaws by the bare skin around the eyes and lores, which is dark.

Spix's Macaw
Cyanopsitta spixii
CITES Appendix I

Description: Overall length is 22 inches (56 cm). Main plumage is light blue but becomes darker on the back, wings, and underside of tail. The head is a lighter shade of blue and its feathers are edged with light gray. The cheeks are covered with feathers but there is a dark gray patch of bare skin surrounding the eye and reaching forward to the bill. The bill and legs are dark gray and the iris, yellow.

Distribution: Formerly found inside the northeastern region of Brazil, in recent times only in very small numbers. May now actually be extinct in the wild, unless a yet undiscovered population exists. (In 1989 three birds were trapped, two of which were young.)

Habitat and Status: Little is known about the natural history of the Spix's macaw and there may be no opportunities left for studying this species. The continued existence of this macaw now depends on the attempts to breed captive birds, of which there are less than 50.

Aviculture: The Spix's macaw is one of the world's most endangered birds and as such could never be considered an avicultural species. Furthermore, those aviculturists who even get to see it can consider themselves fortunate. (There are a few birds now on public display in several zoological parks throughout the world, for example in Brazil, Germany, Tenerife, and possibly other places.)

Breeding: There are now so few Spix's macaws in captivity that there is extreme difficulty in finding even one mate for many of the specimens kept, let alone finding the few birds necessary for allowing the captive Spix's macaws some selection for the pair bonding process. In recent times only one pair is known to have bred in 1988, although a second pair is now reported as producing young in 1990.

Conservation and Aviculture of Macaws

It cannot be denied that macaws are among the most majestic and most visually striking of all living birds. Their beauty, imposing size, and physical structure combined with their gentle nature and intelligence have given them a special place within aviculture and the pet market for many years. Their success as pets has been aided in the last two decades by the developments in artificial incubation and hand-rearing techniques, which have produced a generation of captive-bred macaws that are adaptable, unreserved, and even affectionate.

Many people, however, believe macaws are better when kept as aviary birds, pointing out that macaws must be seen in flight to truly appreciate them at their best. The fortune of macaws as aviary birds has also greatly been improved by the development of accurate sexing techniques and the widespread availability of captive-bred birds, which prove better adapted to aviary life and more prolific breeders once settled. Moreover, successes in captive breeding have benefited wild populations of some of the macaw species by obviating the need for birds to be taken from the wild. Therefore, the trade in wild-caught birds of such species has almost completely stopped.

Therefore, the future of most species of macaws that are present in captivity looks secure, with a few exceptions. The numbers of some macaw species are dwindling as habitat destruction increases. If this problem is allowed to grow unchecked, as time passes perhaps even the status of species that now have large, self-sustaining wild populations will deteriorate. The future of many macaws is directly tied to the fate and future management of the forests and other habitats these birds depend on for their survival. The destruction of the South American forests is by no means a new problem, but over the last 50 years, the logging industry has pursued an intense commercialism that has left large expanses of forest bare. As mentioned elsewhere, macaws are great travelers and require extensive forest areas for foraging and nesting. The vast devastation that has already taken place will soon have dramatic effects: The diminished habitat will quickly lead to a reduction in the number of birds that the smaller area can sustain. Moreover, as populations of macaws become isolated from each other by the fractures in their range, other long-term problems will begin to appear, such as increased inbreeding and losses of genetic variability. This chain of events may already have started.

It is clear, then, that the aviculture of as many species of macaw as possible is not only desirable but essential to safeguard their future. It is also true, however, that in the case of those troubled species that have captive-bred specimens readily available the wisdom of continuing the importation of wild-caught birds (which never settle down properly in captivity) must be questioned and perhaps stopped, except where they may be necessary for needs such as blood exchanges or the better management of subspecies. Fortunately, at present there are signs that soon there is to be a total ban on commercial importation of all psittacines. This is a move that counts with the support of many people.

The responsibilities of the macaw owner can therefore be stated as follows:

1. Whenever possible, all macaws purchased must be of captive-bred stock.

2. All macaws must be cared for with as much time and devotion as the owner can give.

3. Those macaw species considered to have a sensitive conservation status should be kept purely for breeding and not as pets. Also, every effort must be made to pair these birds as soon as they mature to provide them with an opportunity for breeding.

The ethics of keeping macaws as pets at all has been raised by some aviculturists. Although it is true that macaws are among the most demanding and at times the most difficult of parrots to accommodate within the home, the intelligence and affection these large, imposing birds display can be addictive to any parrot keeper who has fallen under their spell. I have already stated that when large macaws start to become boisterous and lose their tameness they should be moved to a breeding situation. As an extension of this, as time demonstrates the importance of breeding captive macaws, perhaps then it may prove to be a good practice for aviculturists to only keep macaws as pets for the first four or five years of their lives, after which time they can turn these birds over to breeding flights.

Wildlife Legislation Affecting Macaws in Captivity

As macaws become increasingly threatened in the wild, more safeguards are needed to ensure that birds offered for sale in captivity are indeed captive bred.

The main legislation that governs trade in endangered wildlife is the CITES agreement. CITES stands for Convention on International Trade in Endangered Species. There are three main categories in which psittacines are classified.

CITES Appendix I: This strictly controls endangered species. Individual licenses are needed for the keeping and sale of any CITES I psittacine which will only be granted if it can be proved that the bird is captive bred.

CITES Appendix II: This restricts to limited numbers but does not ban the trade of birds that are not yet directly threatened but may become so in the future.

CITES Appendix III: This allows the trade of species that are not endangered so long as birds are not removed from the wild in numbers likely to cause them to be threatened.

The seventeen species of macaw are classified by CITES as stated below.

CITES I

Spix's macaw
Hyacinthine macaw   Military macaw
Glaucous macaw   Buffon's macaw
Lear's macaw   Red-fronted macaw
Scarlet macaw   Illiger's macaw
Blue-throated macaw   Blue-headed macaw

CITES II

Green-winged macaw
Blue and Gold macaw
Severe macaw
Yellow-collared macaw
Red-bellied macaw
Noble macaw

When buying any macaw the new owner should try to ensure that the bird was captive bred by a respected macaw breeder. In the case of birds listed as CITES I, each should have a sales license and the new owner should insist on receiving a copy.

Most if not all CITES I macaws are now banded with a closed ring that can only be put on a bird's leg when it is very young (10–14 days old). If one of these rings is present and is correctly fitted (without a gap as is the case with open rings) this in itself is evidence that the bird was captive bred. Rings with a gap, which are fitted onto a bird's leg with special applicators, are useful in identifying birds; but as these rings can be fitted at any stage of the bird's life, they are not proof that the bird has indeed been bred in captivity. I would strongly advise anyone considering buying a rare macaw to consider only a macaw which has a closed ring (with no gap) and has all its licensing papers correctly filled out.

For those interested in helping directly in psittacine conservation, the following organizations may prove of great interest.

The World Parrot Trust
c/o Paradise Park
Hayle, Cornwall TR27 4HY
United Kingdom

American Federation of Aviculture
P. O. Box 5618
Phoenix, Arizona 85079-6218
United States

Glossary

ascarids Family of worms, including intestinal parasites such as round worms, that infest populations of captive birds.

aviculture The pastime of keeping and breeding birds in captivity.

avitaminosis Any disease caused by a lack of certain vitamins in the diet.

bend of wing Area along the front top edge of the wing that is covered by the lesser wing coverts.

bonding The pairing and mate selection process in birds.

candling Technique for monitoring embryo development inside an egg by using a light to illuminate the egg to view its interior.

cere Fleshy area surrounding the nostrils of some birds, as the parrot.

crop Thick, muscular saclike area of the lower esophagus of a bird in which food is softened for digestion; it also serves to hold food for feeding to young chicks or the bird's mate by regurgitation.

crown Area around the central top of the head.

embryo The early stage in the development of a chick inside an egg.

feces Waste matter discharged from the intestines.

feral Domesticated species of animals that have become established in wild populations.

fledgling Young bird that has just fledged or left the nest.

foreneck Area above the breast and just below the throat.

genus Group of animals (or plants) sharing common physical characteristics that make them distinct from other groups.

habitat Relating to the type of landscape and environment a bird inhabits.

hybrid Bird (other animal, or plant) that results from crossbreeding two different species.

incubator Container used for the artificial incubation of eggs.

initial internal pip Moment the embryo breaks the membrane between itself and the air sac within the egg.

iris Circular diaphragm forming the colored portion of the eye.

lateral Situated at, proceeding from, or directed to the side.

lore In birds, the area between the eye and the bill.

mandible Either of the two parts (upper or lower) of a bird's bill.

mantle Area of a bird's body between the hindneck and the shoulders that reaches down to the upper back and includes the folded wings.

mites Small arachnid parasites that can infest animals (and plants).

monomorphic Birds of the same species that have no noticeable physical differences between the sexes.

monotypic Genus, or group, that contains only one species.

nape Area around the back of the neck.

necrotic Area of dead tissue in a living animal.

nominate Pertaining to the first species from which all later variants or subspecies are described.

nucchal Pertaining to the hindneck area or nape.

occiput Back of the head just above the nape.

pip Moment when the chick first breaks through the shell of the egg prior to hatching.

primaries Outside ten flight feathers on the wing, which give a bird its main flying power.

psittacine Any bird in the Psittaciformes order, which includes all parrots and parrotlike species (macaws, conures, parakeets, etc.)

quarantine Period of isolation to ensure that an animal is not carrying any infectious diseases.

Glossary

race Subspecies or variety.

rump Area above the base of the tail of an animal.

scapulars Feathers that run down the back against the inner edge of the wing of a bird.

secondaries Inner ten flight feathers on the wing of a bird.

sexual dimorphism Noticeable physical differences between the sexes in a species of bird.

species Distinct subordinate division of a genus.

subspecies Distinct subordinate division of a species.

treading Term used to describe mating in captive birds.

vent Anus or excretory opening in animals, especially birds.

Useful Addresses and Literature

United States

American Federation of Aviculture
  P. O. Box 5618
  Phoenix, Arizona 85079-6218
The Avicultural Society of America, Inc.
  P. O. Box 5516
  Riverside, California 92517
National Parrot Association
  8 Hoffman Lane
  Hauppauge, New York 11788

Canada

Avicultural Advancement Council
  P. O. Box 5126
  Postal Station B
  Victoria, British Columbia V8R 6N4
Canadian Parrot Association
  Pine Oaks
  R. R. Nr 3
  St. Catherines, Ontario L2R 6P9

United Kingdom

Avicultural Society
  c/o Bristol Zoo
  Clifton
  Bristol, Avon BS8 3HA
Parrot Society
  19a De Parys Avenue
  Bedford, Bedfordshire

Australia

Avicultural Society of Australia
  c/o Mr. I. C. L. Jackson
  P. O. Box 130
  Broadford, Victoria 3658
Avicultural Society of Queensland
  19 Fahey's Road
  Albany Creek, Queensland 4035

Books

Forshaw, Joseph M. *Parrothe World,* 3rd edition, Lansdowne, Melbourne, Australia, 1989.
Low, Rosemary *The Complete Book of Macaws,* Barron's Educational Series, Hauppauge, New York, 1190.
———— *The Complete Book of Parrots,* Barron's Educational Series, Hauupauge, New York, 1989.
———— *Parrots, Their Care and Breeding,* Blandford Press, Poole, Dorset, 1985.
Silva, T. *Psittaculture, The Breeding, Rearing and Management of Parrots,* Silvio Mattacchione & Co., Pickering, Ontario, Canada, 1991.
Vriends, Matthew M. *Simon & Schuster's Guide to Pet Birds,* 5th edition, Simon & Schuster, New York, 1989.
———— *The New Bird Handbook,* Barron's Educational Series, Hauppauge, New York, 1989.

Magazines

United States
AFA Watchbird (American Federation of Aviculture)
Box 56218
Phoenix, AZ 85079-6218

ASA Bulletin (Avicultural Society of America)
P.O. Box 2196
Redondo Beach, CA 90218

American Cage-Bird Magazine
1 Glamore Court
Smithtown, NY 11787

Journal of the Association of Avian Veterinarians
5770 Lake Worth Road
Lake Worth, FL 33463-3299

Bird Talk
P.O. Box 6050
Mission Viejo, CA 92690

Useful Addresses and Literature

Bird World
P.O. Box 70
No. Hollywood, CA 91603

Parrot World (National Parrot Association)
8 North Hoffmann Lane
Hauppauge, NY 11788

United Kingdom

Avicultural Society
   c/o Bristol Zoo
   Clifton
   Bristol, Avon BS8 3HA

Cage and Aviary Birds
Prospect House
9-13 Ewell Road
Cheam, Surrey SM1 4QQ

Australia

Australian Aviculture
52 Harris Road
Elliminyt, Victoria 3249

Australian Birdkeeper
P.O. Box 6288
South Tweed Heads, NSW 2486

Index

Color photographs are indicated by **boldface** type. Ci = front cover; Cii = inside front cover; Ciii = inside back cover; Civ = back cover.

Index

Index

Index

"A solid bet for first-time pet owners"